CORONATION ST.

CORONATION ST.

JACK TINKER

First published in Great Britain in 1985 by
Octopus Books Limited
By arrangement with Granada Television Limited

This edition published in 1987 by
Treasure Press
59 Grosvenor Street
London W1

Editor: Moira Eminton
Art Editor: Ronnie Wilkinson
Jacket Designer: Fiona Carpenter
Designed by: Design 23

ISBN 1 85051 229 9

Printed in Hong Kong

CONTENTS

INTRODUCTION

There has never been anything in the entire history of British Television quite like Coronation Street. Nothing to match its position as the country's longest running television serial; nothing to beat it consistently in the ratings (except perhaps the evening 'News'). Certainly nothing to compare to the hold it has on the public's imagination.

When it's most famous fan, the Queen, came to Granada's Manchester studios to see the Street and its inhabitants for herself, she asked its originator, Tony Warren, the question everyone always wants answered. Where is the 'real' Coronation Street?

'In the hearts and minds of your subjects, Ma'am,' he told her.

And that, quite simply, is the secret of its enduring success across a quarter of a century, in countless different countries with their vastly differing cultures.

It would be inconceivable that the day-to-day doings of working-class folk in a row of small unprepossessing houses in a North country city backwater could lay claim on the affections of millions of viewers the world over if there were not something true and recognizable there for everyone.

Each street has known its Ena Sharples and its Hilda Ogden at some time, the ancient battle-axe and the whippet-tongued gossip. Every family has, in some guise or another, its Annie Walker or its Elsie Tanner, the social climber and the social shocker. In every pub or bar, there has always been a resident Albert Tatlock, ready to rumble on about old values and denounce new ways as the death of us all.

Tremulous spinsters like Mavis Riley always incite the amused pity and vague speculations of their neighbours. And for every one of them there is a Bet Lynch fairly bursting to lead with her chin and other vital effects.

What was so brilliant, so unique, about Coronation Street when its first black and white images went out live at seven o'clock on that make-or-break Friday was that no one before had seen their potential as popular entertainment.

Until then programme planners firmly believed that mass audiences could only be won by escapism. Real events as lived by real people were left to the documentary departments or the few – the very few – 'kitchen sink' dramas which were beginning to filter through from the theatre's school of Angry Young Men or New Wave British films.

Tony Warren believed differently. 'I wanted to show there was a glamour in the back streets, too,' he once told me. 'But of course I wasn't going to tell Granada that. I let them think they were doing something very worthy – which of course they were.'

And so, along with his outline script ideas for a twice-weekly serial, he attached a brief memo. It described in three terse phrases, the Street and its characters:

'A FASCINATING FREEMASONRY, A VOLUME OF UNWRITTEN RULES. THESE ARE THE DRIVING FORCES BEHIND A WORKING-CLASS STREET IN THE NORTH OF ENGLAND. CORONATION STREET SETS OUT TO EXPLORE THESE VALUES AND, IN DOING SO, TO ENTERTAIN.'

Britain's longest running television serial ever was first transmitted live at 7 pm on Friday 9th of December 1960.

●

Since then it has been seen by over 250 million viewers in 17 countries around the world.

●

Coronation Street is viewed by half the nation each week and each episode continues to be in the top five rated programmes.

●

Over 2,000 actors have been employed in The Street during its 25-year run.

●

More than 100 writers have been commissioned to supply its scripts and storylines, including Jack Rosenthal, Allan Prior and John Finch.

●

The most prolific contributor to date is scriptwriter Adele Rose with over 300 episodes to her credit.

●

Actors Roy Barraclough and George Waring share the record for the most roles played in the serial – five each.

It was a tactical masterpiece. A model of brevity and salesmanship. For it encompassed not only the lofty radical ideals on which Granada's chief, the great Sidney Bernstein, had founded his new commercial television company, but it promised the holy grail for which every producer strives: the power to entertain. And to this day a copy of that memo hangs on the wall of the present producer's office.

Tony Warren was, in every way, a remarkable invention of his own devising. At twenty-two he had talked his way into a job in Granada's Promotion Department where he fitted the mould of no executive material then known to commercial television.

As a former child actor he was worldly wise beyond his years. He absorbed all he saw, heard and experienced and communicated his opinions

on it with mischievous enthusiasm of a highly cultured Puck.

To research his brainchild he had scoured the streets and markets of Manchester, worked as a barman, engaged startled strangers on trains and buses in conversation and taken frequent trips to Blackpool Illuminations to mingle with his model prototypes in their ritual annual migration.

The result was the seed of a series that was to grow into the biggest thing television had ever known. For the first time the small aspirations, the obscure tragedies and the petty excitements of ordinary folk were put into the spotlight. Their foibles and their quirks were turned into the stuff of real drama. Before long there was scarcely a home in the country that had not, in some way, heard of the happenings in Coronation Street. But it did not, as we shall see, happen overnight.

My own abiding enjoyment of the programme, however, goes right back to its earliest times. In 1960 I

had not long left home, a small dirt-grimed mill town not a great way from the spot where all this fresh drama was taking shape. To me, therefore, as a young Northern exile beginning a new life down South, those early episodes seemed as real and personal as letters from home. I treasured their detail without quite realizing their worth.

Over the years I have learned to marvel at the communal artistry which keeps the series alive for each succeeding generation, and to appreciate the craft and sheer graft which maintains it ahead of its field without sacrificing the loyalties on which it is built.

The excellence of its achievements have, in its later years, been recognized and rewarded with every conceivable type of accolade and award. The most famous of its characters are, I believe, a match for any of the great fictional comic figures in English literature. Was Falstaff any less endearing than Stan Ogden or Mrs Malaprop more ridiculous in her social pretentions than Annie Walker?

But what really matters is that the Street continues to fulfil that short, sharp charter drawn up by Tony Warren in 1960.

Coronation Street 1976.

THE EARLY YEARS

It takes less than half a minute to measure the length of Coronation Street. From its junction with Rosamund Street to the brooding viaduct that marks the other boundary is a short enough walk for anyone. But a huge step in television history.

The familiar squat row of seven slate-roofed dwellings flanked by the country's most famous pub and most frequented corner store had as its blueprint a street now long vanished. Archie Street. A typically regimented line-up of Mancunian back-to-backs built at the turn of the century.

Had the original title been adopted, however, Archie Street would have had a very different stage name. As late as a month before the December launch the programme was still called Florizel Street. This was Tony Warren's own flamboyant reference back to his childhood days when a highly romantic picture of Prince Florizel kissing awake the Sleeping Beauty had graced his bedroom wall.

Only when one member of the original cast persistently pronounced it 'Flor-Izal' in rehearsals did it dawn on anyone what was wrong. It sounded like a down-marked disinfectant.

The alternative choices emerged as Jubilee Street or Coronation Street. The basis for these was sound and simple. If the houses were erected around 1897 (Queen Victoria's Diamond Jubilee) it was the former; if they went up around 1902 (King Edward VII's Coronation), the latter.

H.V. (Harry) Kershaw who has served the street fiercely and protectively as both writer and producer since the beginning remembers only that the fateful decision was arrived at after a confused night of the Three Harrys – himself with producers Harry Latham and Harry Elton.

A lot of Irish whiskey was consumed and a lot of old Harry was talked before a straight democratic vote was decided upon.

Next morning a memo from Harry Latham's office announced the new title for the serial: Coronation Street.

'I'm pretty damned sure I voted for Jubilee Street,' mused Harry E., gazing at his copy.

'And I'm pretty damned sure *I* voted for Jubilee Street, too!' Harry K. assured him.

Obviously Harry L. had no faith in democracy!

There were, however, other pressing problems. Not least, the sets. In those days with video recording and editing in their infancy, most of the action took place in the studios. The planning had to be of military precision and timing.

It didn't matter much whether the show was live or not; once those cameras started rolling, they rolled right on to the end. Technical hitches could be covered only with crude nip and tucks; proceedings were halted only in the direst emergencies.

Designer Denis Parkin had meticulously scaled down the dingy Archie Street facsimiles for studio-housed exterior shots, its cobbles faithfully painted onto the floor.

Loving care was lavished on the details of the five interiors used to introduce us to the residents. The careless clutter surrounding Elsie Tanner's antiquated fire range told its own story. So did the cheerless order in the Barlows' next door and Albert Tatlock's over-stuffed Victoriana.

The plain no-nonsense comforts of the Rover's Return and the Corner Shop were more difficult to make realistic. Every single identifiable brand-name product had to be camouflaged for fear of upsetting the sensibilities of the advertisers who had bought up space in the commercial breaks. Those were still delicate days in the history of ITV.

But the eternal dilemma was one of storage. Every week the entire sets for two episodes (one live on Friday night, the other recorded afterwards for transmission the following Monday) were trundled out, assembled, then dismantled and stored for use next time.

Small wonder so few changes of scene were glimpsed. Even in these

On the early indoor set of the Street.

10

Unknown teenage extras.

Initial viewing reaction quickly persuaded Tyne-Tees to add the gritty slice of Northern life to its list. But Grade held out stubbornly against its growing popularity for six months as it continued to add to its figures each Monday and Friday at 7 p.m. (it's original transmission slots).

Johnny Briggs, then a rising young actor making a name in the West End and movies, remembers vividly coming to Manchester in those pre-networked days and meeting up with Violet Carson in the studio canteen.

'What are you doing at the moment?' he asked in all innocence.

'She was so amazed I didn't know she was playing Ena Sharples she almost choked,' he recalls. 'They were all so euphoric about their success in the regions, they'd forgotten a big slice of the country had never even heard of Coronation Street.'

Many years later, Briggs himself was adding to the newsworthiness of the Street as its amorous factory boss, Mike Baldwin.

vast studios, space was at a premium.

It was an almighty relief when the refinements in recording and editing techniques finally enabled Granada to establish a permanent outdoor Street location on its own back lot.

Only one lump in this particular gravy: the cobblestones of the new Archie Street look-alike ran in opposite directions to those painstakingly painted on the studio floor.

'We had hundreds of calls pointing it out, too!' chuckles Bill Podmore, the longest serving executive in the Street's history. Nothing astonishes him about the eagle eyes of the devoted Street-watchers after all these years.

Not everyone in Britain was able to tune in to the unveiling of Granada's brave new early evening flagship. Sidney Bernstein's great rival in the commercial companies' television scheduling, Lew Grade, flatly refused to allow his powerful Midland-based ATV consortium to screen it. Tyne-Tees Television also blacked it from the Geordies' screens with a polite 'Thanks, but no thanks'.

Looking down into the Rovers Return.

Meanwhile, those who were able to see the Street liked what they saw. That first episode, slipped into the regional editions of the *TV Times* with an introductory article on Tony Warren, had touched a response button in the audience no one could quite explain. Produced by Harry Latham, directed by Derek Bennett, and with forceful pioneers like H. V. Kershaw already involved in its future scripts, it stood out in bold relief against the rather bland entertainment provided that night – the sanitized medical problems of 'Emergency Ward 10', Michael Miles' vapid give-away quiz show and a stylish Somerset Maugham adaptation.

People sat up and took notice when Pat Phoenix looked into her mirror and sighed 'Eh, Elsie, you're just about ready for the knacker yard.' Not a woman watching didn't know how she felt – and probably not a man watching didn't long to know how she felt either (in quite another way). A *femme fatale* with whom women could sympathize.

They sat up, too, when Vi Carson, resplendent in her hairnet, marched into the Corner Shop to introduce herself to its new owner with a volley of rapid-fire requirements. Never had there been a TV dragon breathing so much dangerous fire so hot or so fast.

It was, all of it, a strangely magic brew. And when Grade's ATV finally succumbed to its spell, it was re-scheduled to the regular Monday and Wednesday night 7.30 slots from which it has never been toppled.

Press reaction to the first episode next day was mixed. It was also mixed-up. While Mary Crozier in the *Guardian* prophesied to her largely liberal-minded, intellectual readership that Coronation Street would run forever, the *Daily Mirror*, that fearless clarion of the working class, could not see how it would complete its allotted span.

'The programme is doomed from the outset – with its dreary signature tune and grim scene of terraced houses and smoking chimneys,' wrote its critic, seemingly never having so much as glanced out of a train window anywhere north of Bletchley.

Just to show how to sink an argument with both feet in the deep end, he elaborated: 'Young script-writer Tony Warren claims to have spent a couple of months going around meeting "the ordinary people" of the North before he wrote the first episode of Granada's serial "Coronation Street".

'Frankly, I can't believe it. If he did, he certainly spent his time with the wrong folk. For there is little reality in his new serial which, apparently, we will have to suffer twice a week.'

One of the many Ꞌniesꞌ in those two reviews is that at one point Granada's executives had hoped to pander to the *Guardian*-class of viewer. They informed producer Harry Latham that a doctor and his family must live at Number Five – 'to give the Street bloom'.

Retorted H. V. (Harry) Kershaw, 'You savages in the South may not know this, but up here in the North, bloom is an unsightly deposit caused by outside influences.'

There was no doctor in Number Five. And if the *Daily Mirror* – in spite of its celebrated Andy Capp cartoons – missed his social 'bloom', the 'ordinary people of the North' certainly recognize themselves at ten paces on a flickering screen.

Yes, there were pubs run by ill-assorted couples like Annie and Jack Walker. Yes, there were Gorgons like Ena Sharples squatting in the corner of Snug bars. And not just in Manchester. When the programme was finally networked nationwide, men and women who had travelled no further North than north Finchley responded to them as the genuine article and even swallowed the quaint authentic dialect of the North West whole.

'Tony's secret was that he was a great observer,' says the Street's devoted Executive Producer Bill Podmore. 'He really had sat in pubs with old men playing dominoes. And he'd picked up phrases no writer could ever sit in a study and make up.

'There was one old chap telling a landlady how hungry he was. He just said: "I'll have that meat pie now before t'steam 'its t'ceiling." That was the sort of vivid language Tony brought to those early scripts.'

Exactly how that little gem translates into the native tongues of Thailand, Greece, Nigeria, Denmark, Belgium, Sri Lanka, Sweden, Singapore, Holland, West Germany, Sierra Leone or Finland is anybody's guess. But at one time or another they have all been treated to pearls of wisdom from Albert Tatlock, Annie, Elsie, Ena and Minnie.

'I've watched the Street go out with Chinese sub-titles all over it and wondered what on earth they can mean,' Bill Podmore says. 'But the laughs still seem to come in the right places.'

> ## '. . . there is little reality in this new serial which, apparently, we will have to suffer twice a week'

In the English speaking parts of the globe where Coronation Street has also roamed, the natives might be forgiven for being a bit puzzled by the quirky idiom. But no. The Street has won legions of fans in Australia, New Zealand, Eire, the USA, Canada and Gibraltar without ever having to bite its broad Lancashire tongue.

Ordinary people, it would seem, recognize ordinary people.

No one connected with that first programme would have staked a farthing on a long run. Not even Tony Warren. His nerves were in tatters after the protracted labour pains between conception and birth. He was just relieved to see it reach the screen more or less intact.

Violet Carson was not even pleased to be one of the lucky few from more than 500 hopefuls auditioned. 'I'm afraid I'm going to get this part,' she reported gloomily to her mother and sister Nellie when she returned home after reading the role of Ena Sharples.

Mike Scott, an ambitious young director at the time who went on to become Granada's Programme Controller, was less pessimistic, but scarcely ecstatic: 'I was asked to read the early scripts and opined that it would do well in the region (the North West of England) but would *never* succeed in the rest of Britain,' he admits ruefully. 'How wrong can you be?'

They all knew they had something different. Something new and exciting. But was it too new and different and was it exciting enough?

The true gynaecologist, midwife and indeed Fairy Godmother at the cradle of this worrisome infant series came in the unlikely form of a giant Canadian called Harry Elton. Elton had been brought over by Sidney Bernstein as part of his charter to infuse new blood into British television.

Annie, Jack and Ena bring Northern grit to Singapore in Mandarin sidetitles.

Survivors of episode one – members of the cast and backroom boys.

'I could talk to him and he would listen because as a Canadian he was basically alien to British life and its roots. He wanted to know about it and had nothing to lose by admitting what he didn't know. Everyone else was afraid of looking a fool,' recalls a grateful Warren today.

However, from the moment Elton charged into the young writer's

Annie Walker, Ken Barlow, Ena Sharples, Albert Tatlock, Elsie Tanner and Minnie Caldwell share a friendly drink.

office to bellow the news that the series had been accepted to those palmy days of international acclaim was a difficult and stony path.

Of the band of fifteen players originally signed up for the first five

'Everyone else was afraid of looking a fool'

episodes only Doris Speed (Annie Walker), William Roache (Ken Barlow), Violet Carson (Ena Sharples),

Jack Howarth (Albert Tatlock), Patricia Phoenix (Elsie Tanner) and Margot Bryant (Minnie Caldwell) survived as long-stay residents well into the 70s, and of them, Miss Bryant had been engaged merely as a non-speaking extra.

Today their number has dwindled to just one: William Roache.

Those triumphant smiles the company wore for its second birthday celebrations give no hint of the bloodbaths, the purges, the deaths and the traumas, both in fact and fiction, that lay ahead. Two years on all they knew was; they were a hit. Half the nation tuned in regularly to watch their saga. Their fame was spreading abroad.

Those demoralizing doubts and fears among the hierarchy at Granada which had followed their first miserable dummy run-through were already a distant memory.

It had, once more, been Harry Elton who carried the day in the face of top brass pre-first night nerves. He'd screened a second trial run-through on sets positioned at strategic points throughout Granada HQ.

Everyone from the charladies to visiting celebrities was urged to watch and fill in a questionnaire with their verdict on the show.

When the votes were counted it was a big thumbs up. The show was on the road.

TONY WARREN

Tony Warren is today a tall, spare and vividly articulate man of forty-eight, living in a modest flat half way down a narrow footpath. Socially the row of artisan dwellings is no more than a rung or two above Coronation Street itself, and this amuses him.

The houses used to lie in the shadow of a great square cotton mill immortalized in one of L.S. Lowry's famous Northern townscapes. Mr Warren is still furious at its demolition, for he is fiercely defensive of all the values he set out to bring to the screen when he wrote the first draft of what he then called 'Florizel Street'.

'I would rather have written Coronation Street than own a Rolls Royce,' he says simply today. Which is just as well, for the material rewards from his brain child have fallen far short of Rolls Royces.

There were, in fact, many black and blank years when this vulnerable, voluble man regarded the whole invention as a deadly albatross fast around his own neck. He went through the torments of alcoholism, drug problems, depression and came near to death. Many friends despaired of him.

Yet, miraculously he pulled through. The bitterness he felt at what was meagre for so golden an egg has gone. The rifts are healed. He is back on Granada's payroll and

his credit as the Street's true originator has been restored on our screens.

He puts those lost years into perspective like this: 'Everyone wants to top their last creative achievement. But for me, at twenty-three, that was impossible. I had built an insur-mountably high wall and I could never leap over it.

'So instead I banged my head against it. Now I have learned to walk round it.'

Like any man who stops banging his head against a wall, the relief and peace he feels is obvious. Today he is a warm, funny and generous-spirited individual who delights in reminiscing about the fringe benefits his early fame brought: the evening spent with Coward, Dietrich and Maurice Chevalier in the Paris flat of Jeanette Spannier; the friendship with the crusading journalist, the late Nancy Spain; the early work he did with Doris Speed, Violet Carson and Pat Phoenix.

'I am magically happy, magically lucky,' he says. 'Twenty-five years on I would be a fool to regard the Street as a monster that gobbled me up. If I ever thought of it as an albatross round my neck I now wear it as a glittering albatross in my lapel. Something for people to see.

'I regard it as having done something worthwhile with my life and I say that because the people who see it tell me so – the Poet Laureate of England told me so!' This exceptional man could ask for no higher praise than that.

Left: Tony Warren today.
Below: Harry Driver, Jack Rosenthal, Harry Kershaw and John Finch – 1962.

15

THE FIRST CAST

Some were practically born to a role in Coronation Street; some achieved their role; and some had their role thrust upon them.

Of the 500 or more hopeful artists with Northern backgrounds who streamed into (and out of) those fevered auditions, only Doris Speed belonged to the first category. Tony Warren created Annie Walker with Doris specifically in mind. True, he'd based much of the character's attitudes on the awesome landlady of his own local, but it was the Speed technique he counted on to bring her to life.

And although Miss Speed was at first reluctant to come when destiny called, she sailed through her lines, flattening any doubts about her suitability, with one of those lofty gracious smiles that were to become Annie's trademark at the Rover's Return. The actor-proof panel was rendered defenceless.

Tony Warren had been her fan since his days as a child actor on radio. He watched her act whenever he could. 'She was the best Judith Bliss in Coward's *Hay Fever* I have ever seen,' he still maintains to this day. And Doris returned his touching tribute by christening her first mink coat 'Tony'.

Pat Phoenix, on the other hand, achieved her fame as Elsie Tanner when she was wondering if she'd ever see a square meal or a round

nought on a pay slip again. In the North this flamboyant, flame-haired lady had been Queen of the Reps; but the lure of bigger things had taken her down to London, where times had grown suddenly tough in the theatre.

No one would have guessed how much she needed the break, however, when she paraded her considerable personality at that trial-by-script-reading.

Ever the imp, Tony Warren had goaded director Derek Bennett to ask Miss Phoenix to remove her tailored jacket (the better to assess how well she would fill Elsie's ample charms).

'No thank you, I'm quite comfortable,' retorted Miss Phoenix with polite disdain. This was Elsie on her dignity and everybody knew it.

'There was really no point in asking anyone else to bother,' reported Harry Kershaw.

'If that boy doesn't shut up this instant, I'll smack his bottom'

It was truculent Violet Carson who had Coronation Street thrust upon her. She had already garnered considerable fame on BBC radio both with her work as Auntie Vi in 'Children's Hour' and as Violet at the Piano in the late Wilfred Pickles' hugely popular 'Have a Go' quiz games, but had grown distinctly unhappy with the way the Corporation valued her contributions.

At which point, the talent spotters of Granada were also in despair at ever finding an Ena Sharples. The trouble was, everyone had envisaged Ena as a scrawny, vinegar-lipped little shrew. Time was running out and there was talk of dumping her entirely.

Tony Warren was horrified. A Northern street without its ancient she-dragon. Impossible.

Then he remembered his early work with Violet Carson. And she

remembered him too. As a highly precocious child actor, born Anthony McVay Simpson, he'd once driven her to shriek across a BBC rehearsal room: 'If that boy doesn't shut up this instant, I'll smack his bottom!'

One look at the formidable Miss Carson was enough to convince them all that Ena had at last arrived. She herself wasn't so impressed. 'She's nothing but a back street bitch,' was her verdict on Tony Warren's gift role.

Harry Kershaw has always insisted that, apart from Ena, most of the characters cast themselves. In many cases this was so. When the unknown Christine Hardman stepped up to read, Warren passed a note to the rest of the battle-weary panel: 'She's very plain, but when she smiles it's like the sun coming out.' She hardly had to change her name to slip into the part of the bright factory girl Christine Hargreaves, while Joan Heath was engaged for a short stay as her doomed mother.

The veteran actor Jack Howarth had scarcely known a week's voluntary 'resting' since he entered the business at the turn of the century, and the character of Albert Tatlock fitted him as comfortably as an old cloth cap. Arthur Leslie, on the other hand, had almost made up his

The line up between rehearsals for the first and second episodes of *Coronation Street* in December 1960.

Valerie Barlow née Tatlock.

16

mind to retire after a lifetime on the boards – until the role of Jack Walker secured him a handsome pension for the rest of his life.

Other characters did not sort themselves out so neatly. Betty Alberge originally auditioned for the henpecked Ida Barlow, but found herself ensconced behind the counter of the Corner Shop. The Barlow family finally consisted of Noel Dyson as Ida, with Frank Pemberton as her husband and her sons played by William Roache and Alan Rothwell, two young men both making names for themselves elsewhere.

The choice for Elsie Tanner's wayward son Dennis lay between two equally talented, up and coming actors, Philip Lowrie and Ken Farrington. The part, after much heated argument on behalf of both, went to the former and the character of Dennis was quickly broadened to accommodate Philip Lowrie's feel for light comedy. Happily, the more gritty style of Ken Farrington was later accommodated by the Walker's son, Billy.

Elsie's family was completed by the former elocution teacher Anne Cunningham as daughter Linda, and the Austrian actor Ernst Waldner as her Polish son-in-law Ivan Cheveski.

Emily Nugent.

'Well, it's only a week, but it's a bird in the hand'

The experienced TV and radio actress Daphne Oxenford was allotted spinster Esther Hayes' genteel good intentions, while Maudie Edwards, a well-known character actress, was signed up to sign-in the series as the out-going Corner Shop proprietress, and then bow out.

There were the usual complement of extras to give authentic background, from whom Margot Bryant quickly moved centre-stage as Ena's cat-loving crony Minnie Caldwell.

Other soon-to-be-familiar faces quickly followed. Eileen Derbyshire had missed out on the original selection through other work. Her audition reading had been broad Lancashire and when Granada rang her back to consider a small role a few weeks later, they apologized for its brevity and lack of scope. 'They didn't think it was interesting enough for me. But I play everything by ear and I thought, "Well, it's only a week, but it's a bird in the hand." ' The bird was Emily Bishop.

Anne Reid was also recruited to keep a niecely eye on old Albert.

In all, twenty-four contracts were exchanged for that first – and for all anyone knew, only – thirteen week run. The date on which they all assembled for the first time was Monday, 5th December, 1960.

It was four days to lift off and life for most of them would never be the same again.

THE MILESTONES

The first words spoken live from Coronation Street went to the actress Maudie Edwards. When Eric Spear's deliberately down-beat signature tune had faded away with the opening credits, the cameras panned in on the Corner Shop, and followed Miss Edwards through the front door up to the counter.

'Now the next thing you've got to do is to get the sign-writer in. That thing above the door will have to be changed,' said Miss Edwards brightly.

It was a master stroke on Tony Warren's part to begin his first script at this point. Elsie, the friendly neighbourhood shopkeeper, was preparing to hand over to Florrie Lindley (Betty Alberge). So we had arrived at a moment of important social change in this community.

Like Florrie Lindley herself, we needed to get our bearings. And Elsie Lappin was just the character to put us in the picture before bowing out of the frame herself.

Ena had held court, interrupting her fusillade of opinions on the merits of Christian burials with a nod towards the confectionary tray. 'Are them fancies today's? I'll take 'alf a dozen and no éclairs. I said *no* éclairs!'

Elsie Tanner had a humdinger of a row with her Dennis over a two shilling piece she thought he'd pinched from her purse.

Annie Walker had treated the ex-gaol-bird Dennis to one of her withering 'looks'. Ken Barlow had been browbeaten by his father, Frank, over the airs he was giving himself at the university, while poor hardworking Ida Barlow had tied herself in knots trying to keep up appearances and the peace.

The inevitable inquest which followed the day's efforts was optimistic on the whole.

'Generally, we decided, we were pleased,' wrote Harry Kershaw many years later in his fascinating autobiography *The Street Where I Live*. 'There was a vibrancy, a "life" in the programme which didn't loom all that large in TV drama. But was that enough?'

As no one that night could supply the answer to this final question the only thing left to do was to go out and get drunk. Which most of them proceeded to do.

Well, we all know the outcome now.

By the time the serial had reached the milestone of its 2,000th episode on 2nd June, 1980 it had become so much a part of the British way of life

that a letter arrived from Buckingham Palace to set the royal seal of approval on events:

'Please convey the sincere thanks of the Queen to the cast and production team of Coronation Street for their kind message of loyal greetings sent on the occasion of their 2,000th episode. Her Majesty much appreciates this message and sends her warm congratulations and good wishes to all concerned for a very enjoyable celebration.'

By one of those happy chances to which the Street is no stranger, the date of their landmark edition coincided exactly with the 28th anniversary of the present Queen's Coronation. And no royal occasion ever went unremarked in its annals.

Two decades had passed. Of the characters who were part of that pioneer band, only five remained: Annie Walker, Ken Barlow, Elsie Tanner, Albert Tatlock and Ena Sharples.

But there was new life to replace the old. In that 2,000th episode the young Gail Tilsley broke the news to her husband Brian that they could 'expect a baby by Christmas'. Mike Baldwin promoted Brian's Mum Ivy

A happy Coronation Street *comes of age in 1981.*

...ur years on . . . and only another seventy-five to a century!

to Supervisor of his factory girls. And Emily Nugent was in a romantic dilemma over the first date in her ill-starred courtship by Arnold Swain – the Street's first bigamist!

An orgy of retrospective critical reviews greeted this landmark episode, though the doings of the Street, both fact and fiction, were seldom far from the headlines.

'In a sense, the success of Coronation Street is the success of ITV,' wrote my former colleague on the *Daily Mail*, television critic Peter Black. 'It is certain that we would never have had a Northern back street serial if . . . Sidney Bernstein had not believed in Manchester as a real place on the map.'

Bill Grundy, the crusty North country journalist and broadcaster, writing in the *Spectator*, analysed that success like this: 'The Street's strength is that, starting from an almost photographic realism, it allows itself a fantastic touch from time to time. But always it sticks to some simple moral rules to which a great part of the audience can relate. It shows people as themselves.

Which sounds to me very much like a formula for ever.'

The following year, on the 9th December, 1981 with episode 2,159, the Street officially came of age. Twenty-one years old and seldom if at all out of the top five ratings for both episodes.

'In a sense, the success of Coronation Street is the success of ITV'

To mark the event that week, Granada's executives decided that as well as the two regular scheduled episodes, they would screen six gems taken from the archives. Each night a page from the Street's history book was turned, Monday through to Saturday.

There was Annie and Jack Walker's Silver Wedding from 1962. Stan and Hilda's glorious 'second

honeymoon' followed and then came the Street junketings on the occasion of the Queen's Silver Jubilee. Len and Rita's wedding day was brought out of the album and to complete this seasonal stroll down Memory Lane, there were their own festivities from Christmas 1972.

The events squeezed into that birthday episode revolved around Bet Lynch's unlikely impersonation of Mavis Riley on a blind date. Hilda Ogden's dreams of upward mobility by moving out of the area were thwarted when the sale of Number Thirteen fell through. And barman Fred Gee's self-seeking wife took a live-in job in the hotel of the man who'd sacked Fred.

For this twenty-one-year old, the key of the door seemed to fit every lock.

The Street has now passed its Silver Jubilee. Old familiar faces are missing; newcomers have filled their places as in streets everywhere.

But, as Bill Grundy said, the formula looks like for ever.

THE STREET

ROVERS RETURN INN

Tel: Weatherfield (715) 2217

The Rover's Return has always been the hub of life in and around the Street. No matter what great historical events or little local happenings engulfed this close-knit community, here was their forum, their refuge, their club and for some, it must be said, practically their religion. It has provided a setting as familiar as their own homes (and for many, in the old days, a deal more comfort).

Here, since the Street was built, they have drunk their ale and chewed the fat in equal measure. Friendships and feuds have been forged or settled; no secret was ever too safe nor reputation too lofty to escape debate in this communal open-house. There has been a solid core of continuity running through the history of the Rover's which is modest yet resilient, and as lasting as the Street's cobblestones themselves.

Jack and Annie Walker took over its licence on the 1st September, 1937. They were about to start their married life together and it proved a partnership both professional and nuptial which endured for the next thirty-three years. Before them, throughout the bleak years of the 30s, the pub had been run by a couple called Diggins, George and Elsie. But with Jack and Annie came the bridge which linked the bygone values of their Victorian forefathers to the ordinary young men and women about to fight a Second World War and get Britain through the austerities of a very different peace.

> **Bitter sells for 64p per pint in the Rovers and Mild will set you back 60p. Lager now costs 78p and Guinness 80p**

Their own offspring, born just before and just after the outbreak of that war, were in turn a new generation who would enjoy the teenage freedoms of the rock and roll 50s and the social liberations of the prosperous 60s. Both Billy and Joan Walker in their separate ways were children of their time and station: Billy with his amoral wheeler-dealing, Joan with her coolly calculated social-climbing.

They belonged to an era of change and adventure, while Jack and Annie stayed steadfast to their roots and obligations. Despite all Annie's borrowed airs and graces, their business was the bedrock of their existence and when Jack died, Annie resolutely continued to rule over their little empire alone for the next fourteen years of changes and different faces. Only when time took its toll on her apparently rust-proof will power did she abdicate her duties behind that bar.

It would, of course, have thrilled both Jack and Annie (for vastly different reasons) to hand down the Rover's through a Walker Dynasty. But it was not to be. Even Annie

Above: Jack Walker.
Left: Annie explains the rules but is Billy listening?

could not impose her dreams on history.

When Billy came back, briefly, to take over his mother's heritage from Fred Gee's temporary stewardship, it was clear to all that he was not cast in either of his parents' mould. The square peg quickly removed itself from the round hole. And two short-lived managers later, a sense of order and family stability was restored.

In February 1985, Bet Lynch – Annie's tried if not always trusted handmaiden – assumed the licencee's crown, Betty Turpin as ever by her side. Continuity reigned once more. Which is, after all, the true secret of any well-ordered society.

In no other house in Coronation Street can you find the quiet face of change across the decades more clearly drawn than here at Number One. For Albert Tatlock took over its tenancy back in 1919 as a newly married man just returned from the horrors of the Great War. The son of a mill weaving family, he was as Lancashire as hotpot; as much a vital part of Weatherfield's little history as the grimed brickwork of the houses themselves.

His short education had been part-time at a factory school; his long life's passion was four years' service in the Lancashire Fusiliers. Yet while he would go on endlessly in the years afterwards about the bloody warfare at Vimy Ridge, nothing ever persuaded him to discuss the heroism which had won him his Military Medal – a decoration only bestowed for outstanding gallantry. To Albert's generation, what was rightful pride in common endeavour was vain boast on your own behalf.

Bessie, his wife, had given birth to their daughter Beattie while her husband, like so many of those returned survivors of the trenches, was out of work during the Depression. The land fit for heroes to live in did not look to be running with much milk, let alone honey, from where Bessie Tatlock viewed it behind the sandstoned front doorstop of Number One.

No one, however, could accuse her husband of reneging on the dogged patriotic ideals which had driven him and his generation towards their first (and sometimes their only) glimpse of life outside the narrow confines of their birthplace.

He soldiered on, and by the time Jack and Annie Walker became his neighbours at the Rover's, Albert – a life long socialist of the old Fabian school – was providing for Bessie and Beattie as full-time Steward of the local Labour Club.

His service to King and country in the Second World War, alas, was restricted to the tame battlefields of Weatherfield Town Hall where he enjoyed the rank of Temporary Local Government Clerk until he retired and devoted the rest of his time to the role of Street philosopher and guardian of public morality – a pastime he grudgingly shared with his childhood playmate, the redoubtable Ena Sharples.

Bessie died in 1959 and Beattie had already moved away and married. So by the time Coronation Street became public property, courtesy of Granada's cameras, Albert was a lone widower, set as firmly in his ways as his views.

However, life at Number One, like life the world over, did not stand still. Soon Albert's amiable niece Valerie was there to look after the old campaigner. With her came the fresh air of romance. And Albert, though he firmly resisted any display of eager approval, could not have been more delighted to welcome young Ken Barlow from next door at Number Three into the family. Here

Three generations of family life in Number One.

when Ken married Deirdre Langton at the end of their tangled courtship, it was to old Albert's home that she brought her daughter Tracy.

Among so many of the old bits and pieces which Albert and Bessie had collected over the years, Ken and Deirdre embarked on marriage. Since when the house has not gone short on drama. First its foundations were fairly shaken, so to speak, by Deirdre's famous love triangle with Mike Baldwin and then, more radically, by the death of the Street's oldest inhabitant, the truculent, irascible, admirable Albert himself.

With him, of course, has gone much of the past, not least the massive old sideboard which dominated the parlour all those years. Yet like that vast monument to domestic decency (it fetched a handsome sum

was the youthful man of university learning and solid Street worth matched up with the old man who prided himself fiercely on his self-education in 'the university of life'.

From then on Albert treated Ken like the son he had never had while Ken, in turn, never failed to give him the affection and slightly amused respect good sons reserve for caring parents.

So close did the two become that when Val died so tragically in their modern flat across the way, it seemed only natural that Ken should move in with Uncle Albert. And

as a prized antique), Albert's own worth lives on. As his adoptive second family prepare to put their own stamp on the place with its first major modernization since the advent of the electric light and indoor lavatory, Number One has come from humble millworker's cottage to a professional middle-class abode in two generations of more or less the same family's life. Bessie Tatlock would never recognise her old home today with Ken's determined DIY transforming the place by painful trial and error.

**Tel: Weatherfield
(715) 5417**

If Number One symbolizes the peaceful progress of one generation after another, next door there is a different story to tell. From the very first episode this was a house divided against itself.

In 1960 the head of its household was Frank Barlow, a GPO sorter. A man of limited imagination, blinkered vision, he neither approved nor understood his bright elder son's ambitions to better himself at university. Had he even suspected that his long-suffering wife Ida was secretly subsidising the boy from her housekeeping he would no doubt have had apoplexy on the spot.

David, their younger son, was far more his stamp. An aspiring footballer, this happy-go-lucky lad seemed to Frank true to his class and his clan.

David Barlow (Alan Rothwell).

However the Barlows' fractured family life was not to rattle the keyholes of Number Three for long before a long chain of tragedies took them in tow. In 1961 Ida was killed by a bus. Next year Ken, too, had left to embark on his brief married life with Val Tatlock. David, also, was not destined to stay much longer, either at home or indeed anywhere else. After his marriage to the Ogdens' glamorous daughter Irma, a little fame as a footballer and a short time running the Corner Shop, he emigrated to Australia with his wife. There, both he and his small son were killed in a car crash.

By this time Frank had moved away to salubrious Bramhall, a

Family trouble – Ken faces Frank Barlow's wrath.

haven he was not destined to linger in and enjoy the fruits of old age. Not a family on whom fortune could be said to smile, the Barlows.

Nor was Number Three to know untrammelled peace after Frank left it empty. Squatters moved in.

And by the time the Street had accustomed itself to the squatters' rights of Betty Lawson and her brood, the 60s were almost over. Orthodox ownership returned, however, in the shape of Audrey and Dickie Fleming, but they hardly left their mark there.

In two years time, Ken Barlow was a grieving widower and Audrey offered him the tenancy of his old home. Not surprisingly there were few happy memories to tie him there. And with his young twins, Peter and Susan, safely ensconced with their maternal grandparents in Glasgow, Ken soon moved in with Uncle Albert.

Not even the newly-wedded bliss of that placid couple Emily and Ernest Bishop however, could obliterate the blight entirely when they moved in. Remember their early recourse to marriage guidance counselling and their fostering those two black children to help heal their marital difficulties? And Ernest's end, when he in turn succumbed to the evil eye fixed on Number Three, was among the most gory the Street has known: murdered at point blank range in a wages snatch.

Emily now lives on here, a stronger and more self-reliant woman than anyone could have suspected during her tremulous spinsterhood. And with young Curly Watts, the engaging educated dustman, as her lodger, calm at last seems to have settled on Number Three.

Percy Sugden holds forth to Emily Bishop and Curly Watts.

Tel: Weatherfield (715) 4329

The Tilsley family traumas have occupied the spic-and-span interior of Number Five since 1979. They came on the extremely hot heels of Deirdre and Ray Langton's explosive union. And no sooner was Ivy and Bert's own housewarming underway than their son Brian was dating the young and deceptively fragile-looking Gail Potter. The scene, therefore, was speedily set for another cycle of birth, marital fracas and death.

Those quiet, ordered and now faraway days of Esther Hayes, who occupied the house back in 1960, and the blameless Minnie Caldwell, who made it her home from 1961 until 1976, belong to another era.

Esther, the middle-aged spinster office worker, had been young Ken Barlow's staunchest ally when we were first introduced to the Street and its characters, always the one

about smooth-talking Southerners by buying the place and installing Bet Lynch as both its and his mistress.

Coronation Street's first illicit love nest was here but not to stay.

Bet's days of wine and roses were not long at Number Five. At the first – or maybe the twenty-first – hint of wedlock from her, lover-boy Baldwin was claiming the protection of wedded obligations elsewhere (falsely as it turned out). With a speed indecent even in these irregular circumstances, he sold the house off cheaply with poor Bet as a sitting tenant.

She soon found herself in the role of a sitting duck, too, in the cross fire of the great Street-divider debate: should Bet stand on her rights and her dignity and remain there, or should she hand the house over to the newly married Langtons?

Well, naturally, when it came to a straight choice between her own best

New life at Number Five – the Tilsley family Brian, Ivy and Bert.

decision to start a new life in Holland, she knew it was all over. At Ray's farewell party, she lit the final rocket. She was staying behind with baby Tracy. Emily's home next door was ready and waiting to take them in.

So came the three new faces of the Tilsleys, bringing with them many more of the old, old stories of ordinary married folk the world over.

The mundane strains of two females sharing the same kitchen was the least of them, since Ivy and her daughter-in-law Gail are at heart two sensible and sane women. But when Brian and Gail were forced to sell their bijou home in Buxton Close to bail out Brian in his ailing garage business, matters have not been easy on other fronts.

Bert Tilsley's death after his long illness was a blow to them all. But Ivy's early widowhood was not eased by her son's defensive jealousy when a well-meaning neighbour began to ask her out. Nor were her homecomings from the factory or bingo made much sweeter by the rumbles of thunder around his own marriage.

Gail's demands for more financial independence and a house met with Brian's refusals to discuss the matter.

After a reconciliation, Gail's problems seemed to be on the mend. However the feeling of neglect returned and Gail found herself in the arms of Brian's cousin, Ian Latimer. Gail became pregnant and everyone, including the mother-to-be, thought that Ian was the father. Divorce was the result. However when the baby's blood group became known, it turned out that Ian was not the father and Brian was! Gail unburdened herself to her mother who in turn told Ivy. Gail realised it was time to tell Brian. However this revelation was not enough to bring the couple together.

Mike Baldwin.

Bet Lynch.

ready to pour oil whenever the troubled waters next door threatened to boil over. And when Minnie followed her here, the greatest catastrophe that occurred (apart from those not infrequent verbal spats with her indomitable friend Ena) was the death of Minnie's beloved Bobby – possibly the most famous cat since Felix or Korky.

Change came thick and, in every sense, very fast by the time Minnie had packed her bags and moved away to share the remaining years of her life with an old admirer from her unsuspected past.

Mike Baldwin was soon confirming all the North's darkest suspicions

interests and the thought of Deirdre's new baby going without a proper home, Bet's sentimental nature was as overblown as her figure. Out she went, tenant's rights or no. In came the Langtons. And the blue touch-paper to a three-year long marital firework display was ignited.

The ever-nimble Ray was quickly deep into a torrid affair with Janice Stubbs, the striking coloured girl who adorned the café. Nor was the ever-watchful Emily Bishop slow in passing on the news to Deirdre, who was shattered. So, in effect, was the marriage.

Though she briefly appeared to be pacified and even acquiesced in the

23

Tel: Weatherfield (715) 8832

For seventeen years, Coronation Street was without a Number Seven. It collapsed suddenly in 1965, a victim of neglect, old age and the constant vibrations of the trains which then rattled ceaselessly across

Harry Hewitt and Albert Tatlock.

the viaduct. And only by a miracle did Lucille Hewitt emerge alive and badly shaken.

She used to go back there periodically whenever life seemed too tough to take, just to remember those happy days before her real mother had died and father Harry reluctantly had to put her into an orphanage.

Lucille was the Street's problem child. But communities like Coronation Street have always prided themselves on solving their own problems. And by the time Number Seven came tumbling around her ears, Lucille's care and education had been undertaken by Annie Walker and her Jack. It was, in fact, the kindly Jack who first realized that his ward was trapped inside.

Harry, the likeable bus inspector, had meantime re-married, and moved with his new wife Concepta, the former barmaid at the Rover's, to her native Ireland. The house had stood empty for two years – secretly visited, as on this occasion, only by Lucille.

Luckily, as so often before, the Street itself provided the men of the hour. Len Fairclough and Jerry Booth were on hand to effect the rescue and then to carry out the complete demolition of the remaining shell.

The gap, left like a missing tooth in the matching row, was plugged by some slight cosmetic surgery: a rest arbour. Cynics might wonder who on earth would wish to sit out there and contemplate the view.

Yet it stayed there, offering its anachronistic shelter, until Len himself decided to capitalize on the fruits of his own labour and acquire the site for some lucrative speculative building. By this time, of course, he himself was married to the strong-minded Rita Littlewood. And she

had very firm ideas about which of the Fairclough establishments she preferred – Number Seven's discreetly upmarket, updated version of the original blueprint or the home next door which Len had shared with his partners Jerry and Ray and where he had brought her as an unblushing bride.

It was no contest. Into Number Seven's gleaming new interior moved the Faircloughs and there they stayed until Rita's dreams of an ideal home crumbled as suddenly and almost as completely as Lucille's had done all those years before. Len was killed on his way to a rendezvous with another woman. This was not a case where the wife was the last to know. No one knew until it was too late for any recriminations or forgiveness.

But Rita was never one to let life count her down or out. She remains in the house that Len built, getting on with her own life and sorting out Mavis's at work in the Kabin where Len had set her up in a business of her own.

9

Tel: Weatherfield (715) 8436

The Duckworths – Vera, Jack and son Terry – are comparative newcomers as Street residents. But they follow an old tradition. They are the brash, noisy disturbers of its respectability and peace, as were the Tanners and the Ogdens before their rougher edges were smoothed away by having to rub along with their neighbours.

When we first visited Coronation Street, Number Nine was empty and remained so until Elsie's daughter, Linda, having patched up her rocky marriage, persuaded her Polish husband, Ivan Cheveski, to move back home close to Mum.

Then it was the turn of the peripatetic Ken and his bride to move in. They turned the downstairs front room into a hairdressing salon, so that Val could continue her trade from home. Their twins, Peter and Susan, came along in 1965 – and bang went Val's pin-curl money.

By 1968, the Barlows had moved on and up – to the block of luxury flats across the road where Val was to perish, adding yet another black chapter to their family saga.

The house, by now, had been bought by Len Fairclough (for the bargain price of £1,000) and he quickly turned his modest piece of real estate into a bachelor paradise. Both his partners, Ray Langton and Jerry Booth at one time or another in their lives, joined him there, though they had about as much in

Ray Langton (Neville Buswell).

The battling Duckworths Vera, Terry and Jack.

common as the hare and the tortoise.

The solid, reliable Jerry died of a heart attack in November 1975; the fast-working Ray left to marry Deirdre in 1975. Two years later, this all-male stronghold surrendered its status when Len himself succumbed to the lures of matrimony when the worldly Rita Littlewood crossed the threshold as the new Mrs Fairclough. She did not, as we know, stay long. No sooner was Number Seven re-built with all its mod cons than Rita had claimed it and Number Nine was sold off to the grouchy Chalkie Whiteley who brought his grandson, Craig, to add some fresh blood to the Street's younger generation.

However, Chalkie was one for the horses. And when a five-horse accumulator romped home to bring in a jackpot of £3,543.75p, the victorious Grandad Whiteley celebrated by taking himself and Craig off for good to join their relatives Down Under.

And so, in 1983, came the clamorous Vera with her corncrake cries and brassy Brillopad hair, and Jack-the-Lad Duckworth with his eyes for the birds, his instinct for trouble and his taste for the main chance. With them, too, came son Terry – a lad well-trained to look out for himself in life. No one sleeps while the Duckworths are around.

11

Tel: Weatherfield (715) 8825

Elsie Tanner, the Street's famous *femme fatale*, arrived here, just as World War II began, as a pregnant sixteen-year-old bride. The tongues started wagging even then. And as Elsie grew older and bolder she never failed to give them plenty of exercise.

If she gave a damn, she was too gutsy and too proud to let anyone outside know it. Meanwhile, wolves of every shape and size were never far away from her front door.

Somehow she brought up Linda and Dennis, coping in her off-hand, brusquely affectionate fashion when her own daughter's marriage ran into stormy waters or Dennis brushed with the law. Which is how we met them in the very first episode.

Mrs Tanner's sundry romances, marriages, exits and entrances kept

Agony Aunt – Elsie with Gail Potter.

The Claytons brought young romance and problems to the Street.

Number Eleven in the spotlight of Street gossip until her last departure in 1984, when Bill Gregory, a blast from her tornado past, swept her off into the sunset of Portugal on yet another sentimental journey.

In between Elsie's tempestuous tenancies, life did not lie dormant. Ken Barlow, with his second wife Janet, alighted here briefly before he finally settled in with Uncle Albert

and Number Eleven was added to the ever-mobile Barlow scenario.

Back came Elsie after the breakdown of *her* marriage to Alan Howard. Not only did she reclaim her old home but her old surname.

The house, with Elsie presiding as a kind of worldly-wise house mother, soon gave board and shelter to other single girls in search of life's adventures: Gail Potter and the wayward Suzie Birchall both lodged here and Elsie with her big heart and the fruits of her wide knowledge, was an ideal landlady.

In the wake of Elsie's latest voyage of self-discovery, the tally of young bachelors in the Street was given a timely boost by the arrival of Kevin Webster. Kevin came with his widowed Dad and sister and when Dad re-married and left the district, Kevin stayed on, thoroughly integrated into Street life as Brian's garage mechanic.

One more tenancy on, and Number Eleven welcomed another family. Milkman Harry Clayton, his wife Connie and their daughters Andrea and Sue. Things were fine for the family until Andrea became pregnant by Terry Duckworth. To escape from the scandal this caused, the Claytons did a moonlight flit, never to be seen again.

Residency was then taken up by newly-weds Alf and Audrey Roberts. Audrey was less than pleased at the thought of moving in, as her sights were fixed on somewhere a little more luxurious. However, Alf had his way and the house was soon under new ownership.

13

(No telephone)

It was, indeed, Lucky Thirteen for Stanley Ogden when he pulled off his one successful business deal and neither he nor Hilda ever rued the day he invested all their savings in the tiny two-up-two-down. The price was £575 – £200 down, the rest on mortgage. Even in 1964 that was a good buy.

What is more, it marked them out as unique in the Street: its first members of Britain's new house-owning democracy. Whatever the

Hilda with bookie Dave Smith (Reginald Marsh).

Hilda (back in curlers!) with daughter Irma.

Stanley Ogden – builder, window cleaner and entrepreneur extraordinaire!

neighbours thought of them – and the Ogdens have given them plenty to think about – Hilda never forgets how she stole this march on the rest. Come what may, she can look them straight in the eye.

A great deal did come her way in the twenty years she shared the house with her Stan but Trevor, their only son, was not often one. He had flown the coop as quickly as he could, only to fly back if he thinks there is a chance to feather his own nest.

Irma, their forthright daughter, was around much longer, a firm favourite. Even when she eloped

with David Barlow, the entire Street discovered where they were having their secret wedding breakfast rendezvous and turned up in force.

Here it was that Hilda and Stan chivvied and chaffed their way through to their ruby wedding anniversary and Hilda's own sixtieth birthday shortly before Stan died.

Over the years, Hilda has tried to impose her own notions of *House & Garden* on the place – her celebrated 'muriel' and flying ducks being her personal trademark. She was, however, not so lucky with the garish lilac paint Stan got cheap and which was still blistering and peeling everywhere after he was gone.

It is all a far cry from Number Thirteen's previous tenants. First we saw the likeable young Christine Hardman coping with her mother's sudden death and her own nervous breakdown. Then came Jerry Booth's brief marriage which foundered on the rocks of money troubles.

The Ogdens were a different breed entirely. Money was never in great supply and when it was Stan invariably squandered it. But only death could part them.

The old place is now as neat as a new pin with no Stan or long-stay lodgers like Eddie Yeats to mess it up. Yet even in widowhood, Hilda battles on. She took on the entire Street in defence of her timid lodger, Henry Wakefield. And when burglars came to Coronation Street while Hilda was enjoying some unaccustomed luxury at the home of her employer, Dr Lowther, it was the electricity meter of Number Thirteen they ransacked.

15

The Corner Shop **Tel: Weatherfield (715) 7217** What you can't learn in the Rovers Return at one end, you'll catch up on here at the other. Time was when most streets were punctuated by this combination of pub and store. Today the corner shops are an endangered species.

Yet come supermarket, hypermarket or Common Market, the Street has remained steadfastly loyal in its custom to this miniscule outpost of private enterprise. So it should. Our very first glimpse of the neighbourhood was here, as Florrie Lindley took over its goodwill from the outgoing Elsie Lappin.

She was warned about the Tanners (no credit) and Ena's temper (no cowardice) and for the next four years she adjusted self-effacingly into the community, giving few cause for complaint.

There was a brief inter-regnum when she left – Lionel Petty and his daughter came and went. And then it was the turn of David Barlow and his wife Irma (from next door) to try their hands at minding the shop and the Street's business. They were 'insiders' and their customers felt at home with them.

They, unfortunately, did not make it *their* home for long. By 1968 they had made their fateful emigration to Australia where David and their baby were to die. Irma returned for a spell at the start of her widowhood, but for the next seven years it was Maggie Clegg (Betty Turpin's sister) who presided among the sliced loaves and tinned tuna fish.

Maggie's life here was not exactly all a matter of tea bags and sympathy, however. She had not long arrived before she was all alone in the little flat upstairs. Her son Gordon had departed for London to make his way as an accountant, while husband Les disappeared into a nursing home to wage the last round in his battle against alcoholism.

The booze won and Maggie divorced him, taking on first Irma as a partner, then Norma Ford as an assistant to help her through. Then she, too, was up and away, married to Ron Cooke and off to start afresh in Zaire.

Gordon tried unsuccessfully to sell the shop to the impecunious Hopkin

Alf Roberts.

tribe led by Granny Megan, but they did a moonlight almost before they'd unpacked. Deirdre's mum, Blanche, stood in as a caretaker manager before Gordon was eventually able to shed his responsibilities.

He sold up eventually to Renée Bradshaw – who immediately caused Annie Walker's hackles to rise by applying to the licencing authorities for an off-licence. Nor were those famous hackles persuaded to lower themselves when Bet Lynch turned (in Annie's eyes) traitor and gave evidence that as the Rover's did not stock wines, the service would be a boon to the district! But Renée survived.

Councillor Alf Roberts got his feet behind the counter, so to speak, as Renée's husband and has remained here since the horrifying road accident in 1980 which killed her. Alf's own anguish was not helped by the memory that Renée died during one of those silly rows couples invariably have when husbands decide to teach their wives to drive.

Not that he has had time to brood alone, as Bet became his reluctantly tolerated lodger. No one was happier when Newton & Ridley's Brewery whisked her down the Street to higher things at the Rover's.

Alf finds romance again in the company of Audrey Potter, Gail's mother. After Audrey has manouvred Alf into marriage they vacate the shop accommodation and move into Number Eleven. The shop flat, empty since Bet left, attracts another set of newly-weds, Kevin and Sally Webster, who begin moves to become the new tenants.

Florrie Lindley.

The Community Centre

On this site, for as long as most residents could remember, stood the Glad Tidings Mission, the evangelical Free Church hall where Ena Sharples acted as resident caretaker and thorn in the flesh of its elders. Nothing short of a demolition order could shift her from her free accommodation (plus coal!), although her weakness for God's good hops and her all-avenging tongue drove Leonard Swindley, the Mission's upright custodian, to paroxysms of un-Christian urges on occasions.

The old place disappeared beneath the bulldozers of change at the beginning of the 70s and its function was dragged into the twentieth century with the building of the Community Centre – with Ena continuing her vigil as its caretaker (with one short interruption) until she caught a passing broomstick to St Annes-on-Sea to act as housekeeper to one Henry Foster.

Apart from the occasional postcard she was not glimpsed again and her voice as the guardian of the

Ena in the Glad Tidings Mission.

Street's conscience is still sorely missed.

Annie's barman, Fred Gee and his go-getting (and quickly go-offing) wife Eunice took her place for a short spell. Then it was the turn of Percy Sugden, the ex-army veteran, to try to impose a little regimental order on the place.

However, for most of its early existence, the administrative headaches of the Centre was borne by Ken Barlow. As the Development Officer he, and his scruples, gave Coronation Street its first official mole: he leaked Council plans to close down local youth clubs to the Press.

It was the end of his career in social work, but eventually led to his future in journalism.

Baldwin's Casuals

Baldwin's Casuals brought the hum of light industry back to this 'mixed usage' area once again in 1976. Smooth and successful, its proprietor Mike Baldwin also brought some very foreign Southern ways to the Street's changing scene.

But as his enterprise also brought gainful employment to the likes of Emily Bishop, Ivy Tilsley, Vera Duckworth, Shirley Armitage, Ida Clough and even Elsie Tanner when she was down on her luck, no one knocked him for long.

B.C. (Before Casuals) there had been two lamentably ill-fated ventures on this site – both linked in one way or another with the unenviable fortunes of the Barlow clan.

When Elliston's Raincoat Factory (1950-1968) was demolished to make way for a small block of modern flats, in the hope of giving the Street a social face-lift, Ken and Val moved in from Number Nine with the twins. And it was here that Val was electrocuted trying to plug in a hairdryer. The fire which ensued led to the

discovery of structural faults (for this was the era of Jerry built concrete blocks) and the flats were demolished in their turn.

Mark Brittain's Warehouse occupied the site next, with Ken employed there as an up-and-coming junior executive. True to his fate, however, he was unceremoniously axed in a round of redundancies and with the handsome compensation he collected, he decided, uncharacteristically, to hit the freedom trail – as a taxi driver!

However, the Warehouse was soon to echo the tragic events at the flats, when two vandals broke in and accidentally set it alight.

Fred Gee's first wife Edna had gone for a minute's rest because she was feeling unwell. She was trapped in the inferno which followed, the second victim of a grizzly barbecue on that spot.

The occasional industrial dispute of female backbiting which interrupt the routine of Mike Baldwin's production lines these days are nothing compared to these troubled ghosts.

Mike with Mr Yakimoto (Ozzie Yue).

The 60's

During its first ten years Coronation Street was transformed from a regionally transmitted black and white picture of working class northern life into a national institution. Its characters became stars, its fans numbered Prime Ministers and the Royal Family. But behind the dizzy success story, as always, there was plenty of blood, sweat, toil and tears.

Before there was time to celebrate the first birthday of the programme, Coronation Street was already something of a national shrine. Not all the worship directed towards its high priests and priestesses was welcome, however. Much of the mystique was misguided and misinformed too.

Violet Carson was to be found publicly rebuking the gossip-mongers. While Pat Phoenix and her screen son Philip Lowrie were found by a posse of mounted police holed up in a Leeds store as thousands of avid fans staged hysterical scenes outside.

It all meant enormous adjustments, both personal and professional, to accommodate the rigours of their arduous work routine with all this unaccustomed fame.

Some fared better than others. Pat Phoenix took to the film star treatment like a swan to the lake, but Philip Lowrie was never easy with all the adulation he received as Dennis

Tanner. As soon as he had secured his future with some shrewd property investments over the years, he left the cast in 1968 and to this day, shuns any public connection with his Street origins.

'I never stopped missing him on the set,' Pat Phoenix told me. 'We were a very good screen partnership and always remained good pals.'

Above: Old favourites pose for a Street birthday photo.

Annie Walker.

However, hardly had their mother and son relationship established itself in countless homes than there was real life drama to cope with in the studios.

Equity, the actor's union, came out on strike for a new pay deal with ITV and slapped a total ban on all its members, apart from those on long-term contracts. This shredded the Street's cast to thirteen players.

From November 1961 through to May 1962 the Street's new producer, Derek Granger (now one of Granada's major forces in drama) juggled the available cast's commitments and the scriptwriters struggled to keep the missing characters alive.

Harry Hewitt was often seen bawling upstairs to an invisible Lucille; yet only the patter of her footsteps on the stairs dashing to and from school kept the urgency of her eleven-plus exam results simmering for seven months.

Annie presided frozen-faced over an eerie public bar, her features kept in tight close-up so as not to show the deserted dartboard area.

And when Elsie returned home to find a chimpanzee in her chair at Number Eleven, this was just Derek Granger's way of supplementing the missing human interest with animal recruits from Belle Vue Zoo.

His equally ingenious ruse of using non-Equity youngsters to flesh out the Street scenes was stamped on by the union, however, when his script-writers started to use them as under-age milkmen and the like. Equity was not about to see the return of child labour in these old industrial streets.

It is Harry Kershaw's view now that the strike's ill wind blew the Street a lot of good viewing figures. New plays were impossible to screen and the public's thirst for TV drama was admirably slaked by Granada's bi-weekly serial.

With industrial disputes settled and the exiled wanderers returned, life settled down for a couple more years. Its stars went from strength to strength. Everything they did was news.

When Lynne Carol took a private trip to the Daily Mail Ideal Home Exhibition in London, looking as little like Martha Longhurst as humanly possible in a luxurious fur coat, she was nevertheless mobbed and asked to leave on the grounds of public safety.

Alas they were not long, Miss Carol's days of milk stout and moroseness. When Tim Aspinall took over as producer he decided on a new broom policy. The 'Bloody

'I never stopped missing him on the set'

Purge' of 1964 was on and Martha Longhurst was among the first for the chopping block.

In vain Violet Carson argued that to remove Martha from the Terrible Triumvirate around the cauldron of gossip in the Snug was like staging Macbeth with only two witches. Martha vanished beneath a silent requiem of cast credits, the signature tune omitted as a mark of respect.

Right to the end of rehearsals, Peter Adamson, now firmly established as Len Fairclough, refused to say the words: 'She's dead.' He'd bet good money there would be a last minute reprieve from on high – Cecil Bernstein if not his brother Sydney.

He lost the wager.

Tim Aspinall soon realized what the Street had lost, too. His hour of necessity was the mother of inspired invention, however. To compensate for the absence of Martha, the Ogdens were hastily conjured into being in Number Thirteen. Jean Alexander and Bernard Youens, the impecunious parents of Irma, immediately established themselves as vintage Coronation Street wine.

It has never been easy, balancing the fictional requirements of the Street against the actual demands of the actors. Yet on such hang these life and death issues.

When Noel Dyson decided she'd had enough of the milk and water Ida Barlow, she was perfectly happy for her character to perish under a bus. There was simply no other way; Ida was not the sort of lady to throw her cap over the moon and run off with a jockey.

As her widower, however, Frank Pemberton's role staggered on for a while. But when the scriptwriters could come up with no better story line than that the aging Frank Barlow should marry the young Christine Hardman, it was plain the well of inspiration had run dry for both of them.

Minnie Caldwell, Ena Sharples and Martha Longhurst.

Above: Among the famous carollers –
Steve Tanner (Paul Maxwell) and Lucille
Hewitt.
Right: Christmas comes but once a year.

In real life Ivan Beavis and Doreen Keogh had fallen in love and married just as their characters Harry and Concepta Hewitt had done in the scripts. The judge presiding over Miss Keogh's divorce from her first husband altered the date of the hearing to accommodate her recording schedule. 'I am not sure that it is not against the public interest to interfere with the due course of Coronation Street,' he remarked.

His concern did not save Harry and Concepta from being shipped across the sea to Ireland however.

Yet in front of the cameras, life in the Street rolled on.

Many and varied have been the writing talents employed to produce the structured story lines (usually three separate strands woven together in each episode) which carry the viewers' interest along from week to week, plus that added sparkle – the X factor – in the dialogue which keeps them entertained and amused.

Tony Warren, as we know, did not stay to watch his infant prodigy mature. Temperamentally he was not suited to the fierce cut and thrust of the corporate muscle which gives the Street its abiding strength. He was contracted to Granada as a £30 a week writer in the promotions department and it was under this contract that he'd submitted the first scripts to the understanding Harry Elton.

It is part of Granada folk lore that he produced the draft twenty-four hours after being coaxed down from the top of a filing cabinet where he'd climbed to make a vociferous protest against being asked to write dialogue for the company's 'Biggles' series. He doesn't deny it.

It is also part of his own mythology that two years previously, he'd sent a script based on a similar theme to Barry Colehan at the BBC.

'For all I know he's still got it. It never even came back with a polite note,' Warren assured me recently.

Yet by the time he left, bruised and more than a little bitter for the time being, the Street he created had become an unstoppable bandwagon attracting untoppable stars en route.

To make up for the loss of Warren's undoubted flair and sensibilities, there came writers of the stature of Jack Rosenthal, John Finch, Peter Eckersley, Adele Rose as well as that fierce guardian spirit of the Street's standards and worth, Harry Kershaw.

With such men and women, all of whom were to enjoy successful independent careers as writers (and also form part of a vibrant corporate group producing scripts and series ideas of their own) it was small wonder that actors of the calibre of the late Arthur Lowe should also find the Street a worthy platform for their individual techniques.

As an actor, Lowe was a master of

The show must go on! Leonard Swindley – theatrical impresario!

the slow-burn timing as he went on to prove in 'Dad's Army' as well as on the stage of our National Theatre.

The writers knew that in Leonard Swindley's guardian angel they had an artist who, like Doris Speed, Jean Alexander, Eileen Derbyshire or Pat Phoenix, could convey an entire page in one expression.

'Arthur was very impatient of

'I'm not sure that it is not against the public interest to interfere with the due course of Coronation Street'

directors who only focused the camera on the person speaking. He knew that the best comedy came from catching the reaction of one who was listening,' recalls Eileen Derbyshire, whose fragile relationship with Mr Swindley rightly earned him a spin-off series of his own. 'He was a very special talent.'

The writers at that time would capitalize on this by bringing him into all manner of confrontations with the recalcitrant Ena in his official capacity as Superintendent of the Mission Hall, as well as bringing him out in prickly embarrassment

under the doe-eyed devotion of Miss Nugent.

It is said, of course, that actors are only as good as their material. But where Coronation Street is concerned, it is difficult to know where the bricks and mortar of the words and story end and the decoration supplied by the actor's art begins.

Certainly the writers in those early days were encouraged to mingle with the artists and develop any of their natural gifts or mannerisms in the script. So it was that Dennis Tanner, conceived and cast as a tough, tearaway, was gradually transformed into the lively joker, forever dreaming up unlikely schemes to hit the big time, which made a national heart-throb of Philip Lowrie.

Since it was deemed that the Street still needed its petty criminal element, the extremely talented Kenneth Cope was brought in as an ex-gaol-bird looking to settle a prison score with Dennis. It didn't quite work out like that.

A chance reaction from Cope was captured by the cameras and the character of Jed Stone was developed over five years as a comic fixture. As Minnie Caldwell's lodger, Jed became the apple of her eye, until he broke her heart by reverting to his old ways and disappearing back to the clink.

In fact Mr Cope, who had in the meantime married Renny Lister, one of the original raincoat factory girls who'd vanished from sight during the Equity dispute, felt that this particular Stone was gathering a bit too much moss. He left to make a splash in the successful Hopkirk and Randall, Deceased series and to concentrate on his alternative career as a writer in his own right.

Alan Rothwell, too, felt he had committed enough of a promising career to the treadmill of the Street. He perhaps had a point when he complained that the men tended to play second fiddle to the women in the series, anyway. But having grown up in the nearby little mill-town of Shaw, he probably recognized this as one of the facts of backstreet Northern life. Certainly he had no regrets when David and Irma Barlow left the Corner Shop for a new life in Australia. His determination never to apply for a return ticket was signalled to the viewers in the inevitable way: sudden death Down Under.

Left and below: Arthur Lowe as Leonard Swindley the pompous draper who brought the first stirrings of romance into Emily Nugent's life.

Only the fact that a character disappears without an appointment with the Grim Reaper (Death) is a valid hint that the door has been left open for a return appearance should the scriptwriters decide to offer an invitation – or the actor change his mind about staying out in the cold.

Sandra Gough's Irma did come back to the Street and Hilda briefly basked in having her daughter back at the Corner Shop. But things did not work out and Irma is once again consigned to the scriptwriters' cupboard of un-used characters.

The limbo-land can be a decidedly mixed blessing in the careers of those who are shunted out of sight but do not remain out of the public's mind. Jobs get hard to find.

Ivan Beavis, for example, became decidedly frustrated by being forever associated with Harry Hewitt whenever he confronted a casting director. He'd been written out in the 1964 Purge and begged to have the character killed off once and for all to stop all the confusion.

Writer Jack Rosenthal duly obliged. He had him crushed beneath Len Fairclough's van during Elsie Tanner's wedding festivities.

In death there is life-after-the-Street, perhaps.

For those who stayed, the rewards came thick and faster than they'd ever dared to hope in the obscure years of striving that had led them to that cobbled street.

Above: Dennis Tanner with Jed Stone (Kenneth Cope).

Right: Irma Ogden and David Barlow.

Pat Phoenix had turned Elsie Tanner into the first glamorous-granny sex object since Marlene Dietrich. By some remarkable chemistry of sex appeal, strong personality and a no-nonsense approach to life, she had made Elsie the idol not only of countless serving soldiers, sailors and young men back home but also their Dads – and more important for her popularity, their Mums too.

When the 250 strong battalion of the King's Own Yorkshire Light Infantry were asked to choose their official pin-up, 236 of them voted for Pat Phoenix. Proposals of marriage came in by every post – and so did letters from women who identified so strongly with her that they either wrote asking for advice on their love life or offered it on hers.

'I suppose Elsie's secret was that she was tough but obtainable, plus the fact that her heart was bigger than her brain,' she says now. 'I think Tony Warren was a genius to have brought a woman like that into the Street. When she used to shout at Dennis in those marvellous spats we had, everyone watching would know that it was the only way she could show her motherly feelings. She didn't know any other way.'

By the time the decade was over, Violet Carsons' seaside home had become a scheduled coach stop for rubber-necked tourists and Violet herself had been to Buckingham Palace to collect her O.B.E. from the Queen.

Another accolade, dear to every Northern heart, was her invitation to switch on the celebrated illuminations as Blackpool's favourite daughter. She turned up with the rest of the Street celebrities and the civic dignitaries to press the button, resplendent in her hairnet. The crowds went wild.

The height of the 1966 Royal Variety Show was the Street's stars performing a specially written sketch, compèred by Margot Bryant.

If it took a little longer for the industry and the arts to recognize the true value of their work, the public was in no doubt about its valuation of them all. When Elsie married her American army sergeant Steve Tanner (a clever device to enable her to keep her name) twenty million view-

ers tuned in. A record even by Coronation Street standards.

Long after the 60s were over, long after the ordinary man in the street had put his seal of approval on the series, of course, their peers in the industry also began to do homage. In 1979 the Pye Television Awards in association with the Writers' Guild honoured them with their coveted President's Trophy and gave Doris Speed a special award 'for outstanding services to television'. (Doris, too, went to Buckingham Palace for an O.B.E. to match Miss Carson's in the Queen's Silver Jubilee Awards.)

Next year, in 1980, the Variety Club of Great Britain presented another special award 'for its unceasing standard of excellence'.

And the year after that, The British Academy of Film and Television Arts gave them the country's equivalent of a Hollywood Oscar with yet one more special TV award.

Throughout the decade the bandwagon continued to gather momentum. In 1966 Pat Phoenix, Doris Speed and Arthur Leslie sallied forth to Australia to fly the flag.

No one could have imagined the razzmatazz the trip would generate. Even before they left, the most extraordinary fans were getting in on the act. Prime Minister Harold Wilson, keenly aware that his slender Labour majority was about to face a March election, was not the man to miss this heaven sent opportunity of showing his solidarity with the masses. Pat, Doris, Arthur and Harry Kershaw, who accompanied them on their mission, were duly invited to sup sherry with the Wilsons at Number Ten for an official send-off.

Jim Callaghan, another confessed admirer, slipped in from next door, and joined them on the doorstep afterwards for the benefit of the battery of press photographers assembled there.

'It's the only way I'll get my picture in the papers tomorrow,' explained Britain's Chancellor of the Exchequer plaintively.

Their arrival in Sydney seemed rather small beer after this. But as guests of the giant Packer empire, whose TV stations were screening the programme, the tour soon took

Above: Elsie Tanner in full flight!
Right: Albert and Ena enjoy pessimistic exchanges.

on a pace and glamour that took them all by surprise.

Melbourne was jumping like a herd of kangaroos to welcome them. From the moment their plane touched the tarmac they were greeted like a combination of folk heroes from Back Home, film stars and royalty.

Even more tumultuous was their reception in Adelaide where, so they were cheerfully informed, their reception outstripped anything laid on for the Beatles or for the Queen Mother, who had left the city quietly only the previous day.

Flowers and gifts were thrown into their open cars. They were taken on walkabouts and grand tours. Their hands were shaken, their clothes were touched.

Pat Phoenix vividly remembers trying to slip away from the ballyhoo for a couple of hours to pop unnoticed into the cinema only 100 yards away from their hotel. A massive police car with outriders insisted on accompanying her every step of the way.

'No one ever gives you a second glance if you just walk on and mind your own business. But they drove slowly alongside me right up to the cinema. I wouldn't get in their car and they wouldn't go away. I've never felt so daft – or so noticeable in my life. Anyone who didn't stop to see who I was must have thought I was about to be arrested for soliciting. I was furious!'

Another abiding memory is of her visit to a Sydney nightclub with the stately Doris. Although permissiveness had not yet permeated Australian entertainment, no one was quite sure how Doris would take to the antics of one spectacular redheaded showgirl built on the lines of the Harbour Bridge.

Disapproval clouded her face as she beckoned Pat to listen to her verdict: 'Pat,' she intoned. 'That girl should be told *never* to wear that shade of lipstick with her colouring.'

Let Harry Kershaw have the last word on that pioneering trip to the island continent, 'Reunited with our friends and families in London, we returned to Manchester and our last Press Conference on 9 April. It wasn't easy to produce sparkling "quotes" on demand from the profusion of memories, we had had a wonderful time, we said. The Australian people had been wonderful. The whole trip could only be described as . . . wonderful.'

Australia 1966 – They came, they saw, they conquered!

ENA SHARPLES

Ena Sharples had no time for authority or what other folk thought. Built like a battleship, armoured in her hairnet and tight-buttoned old coat, she confronted foes with all guns blazing.

Yet she played the harmonium like an angel and her loyalty to those she grudgingly admired was unshakable.

It was, then, this same forthright, contrary woman who would maintain a ceaseless vigil by the hospital bed of her friend and sparring partner Minnie Caldwell and could marshall the normally peaceful pensioners of Weatherfield in a mass sit-down protest against the closure of their club.

It was this same woman who thought nothing of writing to Prince Philip when they threatened to change the name of the Street, yet who also devoted her time and energies to getting a young boy she'd heard playing the harmonium to music college.

And when her eldest daughter died at her home in the Glad Tidings Mission, Ena's unsuspected emotional turmoil led to the shame of a shoplifting charge.

With her two acolytes, the widows Minnie and Martha, at her side and a milk stout at her elbow, Ena presided over the Snug at the Rover's like some carved Cassandra, forecasting doom and destruction.

She had, of course, been tutored in a hard school. Her husband died on their eldest daughter's sixteenth birthday, and Ena was glad indeed of the Glad Tidings Mission's offer to take over as resident caretaker. For a widow not yet forty with two teenage daughters to rear and another World War to face it was a boon. But she never let obligation interfere with her indomitable lifestyle!

In the First World War things had been very different. Ena had tasted the first stirrings of female emancipation when she left the loom at Hardcastle's Mill and enjoyed the life of a tram conductress. Ena, Martha, Minnie and Albert shared their friendships and rivalries right back to school days.

After the Mission was demolished – before Ena's basilisk gaze – she led a cavalier life, arriving and departing as the moods took her. Her spell as caretaker of the new Community Centre was a bumpy ride for all concerned.

But however precarious her fortunes seemed to others, Ena had an ace up her sleeve: Henry Foster! In the Depression days Henry had cheated Alfred Sharples out of a job. As he had prospered, so his conscience had plagued him and one day he sought out Ena to make amends.

The upshot was that Ena had the offer of a luxury home whenever she needed it. And, after several trial excursions there as housekeeper, one day in February 1980, Ena informed the Street: 'I'm going to St Annes and I may not be coming back.'

Left: Ena fights illness – and the doctor!
Right: Ena happy – with a glass in her hand!
Below: Ena lays down the law in the Snug.

JACK & ANNIE WALKER

One sure way to warm the sunny side of Annie Walker: always call her Anne. Then mention, in tones of respect, the Beaumonts of Clitheroe and Annie will positively glow. For her celebrated social superiority over those she deems the hoi polloi is built on her being a daughter of that august Clitheroe clan – plus the fact that her father always wore a trilby hat to work and was never seen in a cloth cap.

However, if you want to freeze her features into a glacial Antarctic winter glare, then remind her that old man Beaumont never rose higher than a mill store clerk and she herself began her working life at the loom.

Mercifully, no husband could have been more tolerant of any wife's *folies des grandeurs* than Jack Walker. Their years together taught

JACK WALKER married ANNIE BEAUMONT of Clitheroe in 1937 and together they took over the Rover's Return shortly after their wedding. Their son *William* (Billy) was born on 8.9.1938 and daughter *Joan* followed on 22.6.1940. Address: Rover's Return, Coronation Street. Tel: Weatherfield (715) 2217.

him that, in the interests of a quiet, harmonious life, Annie's aspirations must be given their head, only to be checked in the direst emergencies or when even a saint's patience must snap.

It is, for example, no use trying to puncture her intellectual pretentions by reminding her of her humble education at Clitheroe Council School; Annie is by now immovably convinced that her denial of a Grammar School scholarship was due entirely to the incompetence of the Education Authority. No good, either, trying to deflate her accounts of an artist's life on the boards; to Annie her starring appearances with the Clitheroe Amateur Society have

To the manor born; Annie lords it over
Maggie Clegg (Irene Sutcliffe).

Left: Jack and Annie Walker – the perfect
partnership.

assumed the status of a Royal Command at Drury Lane.

All this Jack endured with affectionate, if resigned, stoicism, just as he provided an ever-sympathetic ear to the woes and peccadillos of his regulars. He was, in short, the ideal landlord – and, if Annie herself was never heard to admit it in his lifetime, an ideal husband for her.

Of course, being married to a publican only inflamed Annie's already over-heated self-regard. Her position gave her every opportunity to queen it over the likes of Hilda, patronize Bet, blend condescension with custom at the Corner Shop and claim Ken as her only intellectual equal.

But there has always been another side to Annie; probably the one which first endeared her to the phlegmatic Jack. This is the woman who will give a home and genuine affection to the wayward Lucille, who can bring real charm as well as dignity to her brief role as Mayoress, and above all, whose strong maternal instincts blind her entirely to any shortcomings in her offspring. Joan's calculating coldness she puts down to social grace; Billy's moral lapses, she indulges as the natural wild oats any son and heir must sow.

It was, of course, the night of the Great Gas Leak when the real nature of Annie's feelings for Jack were uncovered. She joined the evacuees in Mr Swindley's Mission Hall with her most treasured possessions tucked inside her handbag; Jack's old wartime love letters, carefully saved and tied up with ribbon.

He, in turn, had brought hers.

Annie with Lucille Hewitt.

ANNIE WALKER: '*One of the drawbacks of selling beer . . . one has to put up with the coarseness it engenders!*'

'*My idea of heaven is doing a foxtrot across a chalked dance floor.*'
ANNIE'S FAVOURITE SAYING: '*Chaçun à son gout.*' (sic) (*To each his own*)
ANNIE'S RECURRING ILLNESS: '*I feel one of my "heads" coming on. Migraine, you know, dear. Still, they do say it is a complaint suffered by people of higher intelligence – just an old wives' tale, of course.*'

MAGIC MOMENTS OF THE 60's

□ Larry and Concepta Hewitt were the proud owners of a sleek greyhound 'Lucky Lolita'. In February 1962 the dog's racing career was launched with a race at White City and the entire Street took the trip for its début. To their delight 'Lucky Lolita' romped home. Gold fever struck Coronation Street as a result for the dog's second outing. Every brass farthing they could scrape together was staked, including Elsie Tanner's entire holiday savings. 'Lucky Lolita' lost – and unlucky Elsie stayed at home.

□ One of Dennis Tanner's efforts to entertain the neighbourhood was a full-scale version of 'This Is Your Life' in the Mission Hall. The mystery victim turned out to be Annie Walker, whose thrill at so much undivided attention directed to her life and good works was somewhat blunted by the appearance of the garrulous old drayman who'd guided her horse when she graced the 1933 Clitheroe Co-op Carnival Parade as Lady Godiva – dressed only in a body-stocking and a long blonde wig.

□ In September 1963 an unprecedented drama arose behind the cameras. An episode, already filmed, had to be abandoned at the last minute. The offending scenes showed Sheila Birtles (a local factory girl, crossed in love) committing suicide by gassing herself after taking an overdose of aspirin. Before it could be screened, however, someone leaked the story to the Press. Such an outcry ensued that the IBA itself stepped in. What viewers actually saw was Dennis Tanner becoming the hero of the hour breaking into her room and bringing her round.

□ Ena Sharples had got her own way at the Mission for most of the thirty years she'd lived there. But when it was sold for redevelopment, not even Ena could stem the tide of progress. In the depths of January 1968, she was evicted. For once she was powerless against authority's might and this unaccustomed role made her seem somehow very vulnerable. The sight of her standing there in hairnet and pinny, like some female Canute silently defying the waves, as the builders moved in to tear down her home left no eye dry.

□ Young Ken Barlow got past the holding-hands stage of love affairs early in 1961 with Marion Lund (Patricia Heneghan), the 33-year-old librarian from his university. Ida, ever the mother-hen, was horrified. She had helped finance him through university from her earnings at the Imperial Hotel to learn other things than the facts of life. The Older Woman, however, found Ken a bright pupil.

☐ Annie Walker was entirely satisfied with the results of the brewery's 'Perfect Landlady' competition. She'd won it – plus a holiday for two in Majorca. Jack, of course was too busy holding the fort, so Ena volunteered her services. To her amazement Annie lived up to the new title and took her. Ena rewarded her by returning to spread the gossip that Annie had stayed on 'because of a man' . . . She was in fact negotiating with the brewery for Jack and herself to take over their island hotel.

☐ The darts team's outing in 1963 was not old soldier Albert Tatlock's finest hour. The demon drink took hold before the night was through and Albert remembered little of how he and Alf Roberts came to be charged with assaulting a police officer in the execution of his duty. But when Alf was fined £5, he counted himself lucky with the token 50p penalty imposed because of his great age.

□ There was little Stan Ogden wouldn't do to earn a quick and easy fiver. But wrestling with professional grunt-and-groaner Ian Campbell was only quick. Oggie the Terrible was flung ignominiously out of the ring. When he'd shelled out for the helpers, the 50p profit he had left over scarcely covered the bruises. It was the end of another career.

□ Everyone was stunned when, in April 1966, Ena was charged with shoplifting in the Pick-a-Snip supermarket. She and Minnie were hauled to the manager's office and confronted with the unpaid-for items. Ena steadfastly protested her innocence and the court accepted that she was still confused and grieving over the sudden death of her daughter Vera in the Mission Vestry.

□ It was Leap Year in 1964 and Emily Nugent, being an old-fashioned girl, believed in tradition. Very formally she proposed to the man of her dreams, Leonard Swindley. He blushingly accepted and for a time they were chastely betrothed.

The 70's

The durability of Coronation Street during the 70's was to be severely tested by deaths, disagreements and defections. Several of the familiar favourites who had survived the first decade succumbed to one or other of these fates as the programme continued to beat off all challengers in the ratings battle. Time had proved its worth, but age had become its enemy.

Ten years is a long time in anyone's life.

A decade under the remorseless glare of often unwelcome publicity plus the discipline needed to survive the gruelling weekly schedules of television's already longest running serial was taking its toll on the old brigade of regulars. More and more producers and writers were having to accommodate the personal crises of the actors and tailor their scripts accordingly.

When Harry Kershaw, back in the halcyon days of their triumphant Australian tour, was asked at a Press conference if Coronation Street could survive without its stars he'd replied: 'There are no stars in Coronation Street.'

To which Pat Phoenix, speaking up on behalf of her colleagues, had politely interposed: 'What Mr Kershaw means is that in Coronation Street we're *all* stars!'

In many ways both were equally right, but Harry Kershaw was more right than the others. Throughout the 70s and much of the 80s Coronation Street has been forced to survive without the characters on whom its fame was founded. 'It'll never be the same without so-and-so,' people would say. But so-and-so went, and it was.

Arthur Leslie, as greatly loved an actor as his character, Jack Walker, was a landlord, died suddenly at the beginning of the decade, leaving Doris Speed without her straightman. Their perfectly timed double act behind the bar of the Rover's was, in its way, as celebrated as that of Morecambe and Wise. Yet the Rover's remained the natural centre of Street life and Annie continued to hold court there supremely.

Right: Lucille Hewitt.

Albert's 80th birthday.

Jennifer Moss was a casualty of another kind. Almost from the outset, young Lucille Hewitt had enthralled half the nation with her growing pains; but Miss Moss had also been undergoing some painful adjustments on her own account. Virtually self-supporting since she joined the cast straight from school at the age of sixteen, and fixed in the mind of the public as a gymslipped schoolgirl six years her own junior, she had plunged headlong into some extremely ill-judged over-compensating for a frustrated youth. Fast cars, a luxury home, a broken marriage after a whirlwind courtship to a gangling youth several years her junior, a severe miscarriage and the birth of a premature daughter had left her with more personal problems than she could handle. By the time little Lucille Hewitt was ripe for character development in the scripts, Jennifer Moss was unable to cope with her own life story. Another familiar face was lost.

So for many years was Miss Moss's private and professional life. But by a happy coincidence as Thelma Barlow and I were lunching in the club used almost exclusively by Granada folk, there she was looking fit and happy and putting in a few days work for one of Granada's drama projects. The two women greeted each other with real affection.

Violet Carson was always something of a law unto herself. As the years rolled by, she could be coaxed from the comfort of her home near Blackpool on fewer and fewer occasions. There was an entire year in the 70s when she did not put in an appearance; only some ingenious references on the part of the writers kept Ena's unseen presence brooding in the Snug.

When she did agree to film, of course, they made sure that their famous asset made maximum impact on her fans.

But perhaps there was an element of sly revenge on someone's part when Ena was made to veto a planned trip to Blackpool (Vi's beloved home town) with Minnie and insisted on staying in the Street and doing the spring cleaning instead. The ladies sat in the backyard consuming the picnic they should have eaten on the sands at Blackpool – and Minnie wore her spring hat as a silent rebuke.

An added irony to this ruse of keeping Miss Carson away from a tempting day's filming on her own doorstep was that, when the cameras were not turning, the two ladies were never the best of bosom buddies.

In order to prevent any of these backstage headaches communicating themselves to the viewers, therefore, the Street has always liked to show its community spirit in action. Any excuse to celebrate and get the bunting out.

Albert Tatlock's eightieth birthday came in very handy to show a united front and welcome any newcomers into the family fold. The man responsible for keeping track of the birth, marriages, deaths and anniversaries in the Street is the remarkable Eric Rosser. So complex is the task that he is the official archivist to the programme and a vital link with its past in all the heated script conferences.

'We realized very early on that the public identify as closely with the characters as they do, sometimes, 47

Emily Nugent – ever shy and ladylike.

Ernest Bishop with Emily Nugent.

with their own families. Woe betide us if we'd let Albert's eightieth go by without a party!' he chuckled.

'The reason characters survive in the Street is that the artists themselves are able to bring something special that the writers and producers recognize and can capitalize on,' explained Bill Podmore, who as the Street's longest serving Executive Producer has seen more artists come and go than anyone.

By the early 70s for example, the Ogdens, Miss Nugent and Len Fair-clough had all stepped up from the periphery of life in the Street and become vital clogs in its smooth running. So, when lynchpins like Jack Walker sadly slipped away, the show still rolled merrily along.

Eileen Derbyshire remembers the precise moment when Emily began to pull her socks up and look the world in the eye.

'Two of the girls in the Rover's hatched a plot to introduce her to a man. For a joke they persuaded her to have her hair done in the latest style. It was the days of beehives and flounced skirts and Emily got herself all dolled up. Now I think it is very unlikely that a woman – even Emily – having seen herself look like that would go right back to never taking any trouble with her appearance again.'

And so we saw the writers bring Emily to full bloom until she was ripe to marry her spiritual counterpart, Ernest Bishop. On paper it should have been a marriage made in heaven. But when Stephen Hancock came to bow out of the cast, the writers had to think carefully about Emily's ''till death do us part' vows.

Ernest was a lay preacher. He couldn't simply run off with the cub mistress (although in real life the Sunday papers tell us otherwise every week).

Thus, a murder was arranged – and Emily was again a woman alone.

'But she couldn't simply go on being a jelly after coming through all that, could she?' laughs Miss Derbyshire.

It was the ever-watchful Bill Podmore who pointed out how his team of writers had solved the problem of filling Emily's worn-out slippers. 'The original Emily character is really Mavis now. And that lovely partnership between Mavis and Rita is, on a different level, a subtle variation on the wonderful relationship we had between Emily and Mr Swindley back in the 60s.'

Controlling the destinies of the characters in the Street would seem to be a never ending game of Musical Chairs and Unhappy Families.

After Anne Reid indicated in 1971 that she wished Val Barlow to be written out, the writers spent the next ten years exercising their imaginations on behalf of the bereaved

Ken. A stalwart of the series, he had to be kept in the forefront of the action.

Their solutions were, to say the least, diverse. Ken was given a dizzy whirligig of romances. If handled by an actor of a different temperament to William Roache, these would surely have seduced him into thinking himself Coronation Street's answer to Warren Beatty.

There was a pretty hotel receptionist whom he tried to turn into a carbon copy of Val. Then, amazingly, there was Rita Littlewood. She turned up at his school calling herself 'Mrs Bates' and claiming to be the mother of her live-in lover's son, a pupil of his; Ken's headmaster nip-

Right:
Deirdre with baby Tracy.

Below: The man with whom she was to find happiness and security – Ken Barlow.

ped that in the bud. Next, inevitably, came the headmaster's own daughter (stunningly played by Joanna Lumley), whose beauty was almost exceeded by her brains.

Turned down here, he quickly

diverted his attentions to poor Norma (Diana Davies) at the Corner Shop who asked him to give her English lessons. This relationship ended on a quaint note. The writers had decided Ken would read her a poem explaining his muffled feelings towards her. No such poem could be found! So Harry Kershaw set to and divested himself of the following romantic gem, signing it 'John Graham.'

'To talk with you
To walk, your hand in mine,
Through well-remembered woods
And watch the sunlight searching
*   through the trees*
To find your eyes.

Such are the pleasures of my life
To be with you
To feel your thoughts, unspoken,
Meet with mine
And lead our lips and eager hands
To mutual delights.
These are my pleasures too.
But doubts arise
To mist those woods and cloud those
*   eyes.*
For, without love,
All pleasures die
And soon the last remaining pleasure
*   is goodbye.'*

After delivering this impressive brush-off, Ken went on to his short-lived marriage with Janet Reid (Judith Barker) and various other affairs with married lecturers, lady trade union officials, and even

Above: Emily with Lucille.

Top right: Val Barlow with Ena Sharples.

Right: Lucille facing Elsie Tanner.

Below: Hilda and Irma Ogden.

Albert's chiropodist. But before this could happen the public relations people had some swift talking to do. Callers demanded to know where they could find John Graham's poem, who was he, and what else had he written? They were told he was an obscure eighteenth-century Scottish poet who died leaving only this one known work for his immortality.

Meanwhile, Bill Podmore's writers were busy stripping down Deirdre Langton's tottering marriage to Ray after the birth of baby Tracy in view of Neville Buswell's request to be released from his contract. It was, of course, comparatively easy to give the irresponsible Ray a bolt hole in Holland, rather than a hole in the head.

On this front the decks were all clear for the Ken and Deirdre dramas of the 80s.

The script machine which manufactures the seamless stream of stories and events each week, year in, year out, is a well regulated but temperamental beast. Its habits are as predictable as the seasons, but its moods as variable as the weather.

There are, on average, nine full-time scriptwriters, plus two assigned to the story line who keep the former supplied with two or even three strands of narrative for each episode.

'We usually recruit our writers from the North,' explains Podmore. 'Not through any narrow chauvinism but simply because we've tried importing writers from elsewhere – good ones, too. But it takes them too long to get their ear accustomed to the real native language of the place. And if we're not for real, we're for nothing.'

Every third Monday all these diverse talents meet, along with the Street's official historian Eric Rosser, to thrash out the details of six future episodes, covering the three weeks until the next story line conclave.

Their deliberations are neither so straightforward nor elegantly conducted as you might imagine. For a start there are twenty-four contract actors to consider, and each contract ensures the artist a specific number of appearances in the programme per year, plus a specific number of weeks off.

It is, therefore, vital that if the team are considering, say, the return of Sandra Gough to the series by bringing back the widowed Irma from Australia, they must time it when Jean Alexander is not enjoying her contractual rest weeks or else come up with a good reason for Hilda's absence.

As well as their own, often highly individual, ideas up for discussion throughout the day, the meeting also considers the suggestions put forward by the actors themselves –

usually out of frustration when their guaranteed appearances have been limited to ordering a gin and tonic in the Rover's, or waving to other actors from their front door.

'A great deal of heat is generated at these meetings,' admits Podmore, and he clearly relishes the fact. 'The time when we start having gentlemanly discussions like some self-satisfied club committee is the time we start producing dull and complacent programmes. The secret of the Street's success is, in part, that everyone connected with it cares passionately about it.'

'A great deal of heat is generated at these meetings'

The outlines run three months ahead of transmission. So, of course, there is many a slip twixt the cup of inspiration and the lips that deliver the lines, as in the Sheila Birtles affair.

Armed with these outlines, the producer then commissions six of his regular writers to turn in one episode of dialogue each based on the stories

agreed upon. Continuity details, character development and the like are all thrashed out at a regular Thursday commissioning conference at which Eric Rosser's invaluable treasure trove of background information is thoroughly rifled. It would never do for Elsie to be seen laughing and drinking in the Rover's with Lucille if they've still not made up the row they had three or four weeks back. Nor would Miss Nugent be welcome in Lucille's presence if she'd just delivered one of her homilies on teenage behaviour.

The writers have two weeks to complete their scripts. Armed with these and the list of characters scheduled to appear, the producer can then only sit back and prey that no act of God, affair of the heart, affection of the liver, or simple traffic accident robs him of one or more before the last shot is safely in the can.

Graham Haberfield's sudden and tragic death was a dreadful blow, both professional and personal, to all in the Street. For although Graham's swashbuckling personality was very different from Jerry Booth's shy anxiety to please, he was universally liked for both himself and his professionalism.

Jerry Booth and Billy Walker – longtime friends and partners.

Pat Phoenix's life also became inextricably entangled with Elsie's fictional story when she fell in love with and subsequently married Alan Browning, the actor playing her screen husband. In 1973 she asked for them both to be written out and Elsie's role was reduced to a skeleton occasionally heard rattling for the next three years.

The actors usually study their new scripts over the weekend after recording two episodes on Fridays.

Monday morning for them is usually free unless they're involved in outside location filming. They gather at 2 p.m. that day to begin the laborious and often boring process in a special Rehearsal Room where plastic tape on the floor meticulously marks out the boundaries of the sets they will be using and the furniture inside them.

This is pure mechanics. The director has to work out in minute detail his camera angles, and at this point the cast are no more than pieces on a chess board being moved here and there for maximum effect and efficiency. There are, in the fifty minutes drama to be taped, over 200 camera shots distributed among three cameras. And it would never do for example if Ena's bulk were to block out Albert's reaction in some dramatic family discussions. Each of those shots has to be carefully composed.

From 10.30 a.m. to 5.30 p.m. on Tuesday is the day for 'motivation', when the actors get to grips with the script and come up with suggestions. If the producer and director agree, the writers will be called in to make the running repairs.

By Wednesday morning, rehearsals are thoroughly warmed up. The actors are familiar with their lines, their moves and their timing. Then at 2.15 comes the crucial technical run. Lighting is planned; the technical supervisor, the senior cameraman and the sound director all assess their separate requirements for

Alan Howard – Elsie Tanner's third husband.

tomorrow's full-scale dress run through.

Once more the actors are reduced to the roles of pawns on a chess board and boredom is the major enemy. There is a great deal of sitting about to be done and various rituals have evolved to combat the languor that can set in during the times they are not needed.

These enforced 'rests' plus the sudden demands to pull out all the stops at a moment's notice for the cameras, are, for some, a dreadful pitfall, however.

Peter Adamson, as Len Fairclough, had become an integral part of the Street family. But while others in the cast whiled away those deadening waiting hours between scenes in their various ways, he blotted them out with the bottle.

It was Harry Kershaw, then producing the show, who jolted him out of the downward drift through the second stages of chronic alcoholism and ensured that Len's presence throughout the 70s was guaranteed by a fit and tee-total Adamson. His plan was to suspend Adamson without pay as soon as the three month story lines involving Len had been completed. Granada would pick up any medical bills entailed in any treatment necessary.

The improvement began immediately. The suspension threat was carried only so that the treatment could be continued and the lesson driven home. He was back on top form whenever the cameras rolled.

On Wednesday night the sets (usually five) are moved in, erected and arranged. And by Thursday morning all is set to tape and time the separate scenes. As on a film set, these are seldom recorded consecutively to follow the story line. The polished editing techniques have freed them from the restrictions of the early 60s when the cameras would roll and nothing could stop them short of a total blackout.

Come Friday, from 10 a.m. to 6.30 p.m. the jigsaw is meticulously pieced together as the scenes are perfected, taped and timed. It only then remains for all concerned to go out into the night and either burn off the excess adrenalin or crawl home and rest.

HILDA & STAN OGDEN

To Hilda Ogden it was as plain as the plaster ducks on her 'muriel' that one day her Stanley would succumb to the wiles of some scheming woman. For her there was no doubt about his fatal attraction to the opposite sex.

She, of course, knew him to be a work-shy, shiftless lump, kept in beer money and cigarettes by her slaving from dawn till dusk at her three thankless jobs. No tongue was ever more waspish than when Hilda deemed it necessary to sting Stanley into action.

But woe betide anyone outside Number Thirteen who dared to point out his shortcomings.

So when her darkest suspicions were finally confirmed and Stan was revealed as the wooer of a fancy woman, Hilda's action was swift and terrible. If her Stanley was dallying on his window cleaning at 19 Inkerman Street (Hilda never dignified its occupant with any name other than '19 Inkerman') he must be saved from himself.

Thus it was that a protesting Annie Walker found herself landed with hapless Stan as a cleaner, while Hilda commandeered his round.

By the time the dust settled in every sense, however, Hilda was almost triumphant that her Stanley had at last been recognized as the Street's Lothario, the last of the red hot lovers.

For Hilda, in her warm impulsive heart, is no less a romantic than her arch-detractor, Annie. That 'muriel' is her passport to domestic glamour. Those curlers are kept in place in case life ever hands her the bowl of cherries she longs for; it will not find her unprepared. The clairvoyant tea-readings are her bid to tame an elusive future, to make sense of fate and not least to claim the oracle's limelight.

Of course she knows what the rest of them say behind her back. But thanks to her Stanley, she can turn round and look them all in the eye. Weren't the Ogdens the very first home-owners in the Street? Their deposit was scraped together from one of Stan's lucrative spells as a long-distance lorry driver and the mortgage repayments cleared in

HILDA OGDEN (née Crabtree)

BORN: 2nd February, 1924
PARENTS: Arnold and Florence Crabtree (sister to Archibald and Norman) of Silk Street, Weatherfield.
EDUCATION: St Joseph's Elementary School (left at fifteen)
MARRIED: Stanley Ogden, 4th December, 1943
CHILDREN: Freda (Irma), 28th September, 1946. Trevor, 8th March, 1949
GRANDCHILDREN: Damian (1972). Jane (1976)

STANLEY OGDEN

BORN: 17th May, 1918
PARENTS: His father was Isiah Ogden and his mother was Mary Pearson. His father was a shipyard worker, of 7 Dock Street, Weatherfield.
EDUCATION: Bessie Street School (left at fourteen)
CAREER: Various labouring jobs and casual employment. Heavy goods driver 1946-1964. Occasionally self-employed.
WAR RECORD: Obtained HGV licence in the RASC 1941-1945
MARRIED: See Hilda Ogden

1965 thanks to her frugal schemings.

Hilda is a born fighter. A proud little bantam hen tirelessly pecking around the yard for all the grains the others might have missed.

On his part, there was nothing Stan would not try to do to earn the quickest quid with the least effort: anything to still Hilda's nagging tongue, but inevitably doomed from the outset and all too often finding the only sympathetic ear was hers.

Throughout it all, Hilda's touching faith in his prowess never wavered. Well, not in public. Only look at the slogan she invented to win their famous 'Second Honeymoon from Loving Cup Shandy'. It says more about her rose-tinted view of their relationship than a dozen Barbara Cartland novels: 'BE A MISTRESS AS WELL AS A WIFE AND YOUR HUSBAND WILL ALWAYS BE YOUR BOYFRIEND.'

The Oggies enjoy a lively chat!

ANNIE WALKER

In common (if she'll pardon the expression) with all the greatest female figures of English comedy, from Mrs Malaprop to Lady Bracknell, Annie Walker sets herself up magnificently to be put down. Her towering social pretentions are built on such shifting sands that one turn of the tide is enough to bring them toppling around her.

With no Jack to curb her now, the 70s found her a constant prey to her own worst impulses.

There was the black day in February 1976 when the TV licence detector vans roamed the district. While the feckless Hilda, forewarned and forearmed, scuttled off to cover her tracks by buying a new one before the inevitable knock on the door of Number Thirteen, Annie remained loftily unconcerned. Like Caesar's wife, she deemed herself above suspicion. Unfortunately, unlike Caesar's wife, when her licence was indeed suspected, she was found to be three months behind in its renewal. The brand of a common criminal burnt deep into her soul.

The Jubilee pageant rewarded her no more handsomely. There she was, centre-stage on the brewery float in the raiments of Good Queen Bess, the personification of Majesty Enthroned. But, alas for royal progress, the lorry would not start. The entire tableau of *Britain Through the Ages* engaged in an undignified scramble to the park, where Annie's discomfort was complete. Bet, swathed in bed linen as Brittania, caught the judges' eye and was 'highly commended' while Elizabeth The Great personified went totally unremarked.

Her regal aspirations took another swipe when Eddie sold her a length of 'personally monogrammed' carpet, only for Bet, quite literally, to pull it out from under her. The barmaid's gimlet eye had recognized its imperious 'A.W.' motif as identical to that gracing the Alhambra Weatherfield Bingo Hall – where Eddie first got it as an unwanted off-cut.

But perhaps the messiest social cowpat into which Annie inadvertently placed her foot was the one which marred her elevation to Weatherfield's First Lady. The cheque with which she grandly paid for her mayoral celebrations bounced. Billy, it transpired, had been dipping into her funds to finance his gambling and even Annie's maternal indulgence finally snapped.

She sacked him as her manager immediately. But this was one comeuppance which cost her a lot more than loss of face or dented pride. It cut deep. Billy packed his bags and disappeared from view for the next five years. If, however, she was wounded, no one had the pleasure of seeing the pain. Like a true daughter of the Beaumonts of Clitheroe, she sallied forth as Alf's Mayoress as if to the manor born.

This is the magic mixture of pure mettle and human fallibility which endears Annie Walker to her public and secures her place among Britain's gallery of Greats.

Annie Walker – Queen of the Rovers Return.

Sisters under the skin?

ANNIE WALKER

BORN: 11th August, 1909 at Clitheroe
PARENTS: Edward Beaumont (mill store clerk) and Florence (née Scattergood)
EDUCATION: Clitheroe Council School
MARRIED: Jack Walker, 1937 (widowed 30th August, 1970)
HOBBIES: Amateur Dramatics (a memorable Lady Godiva in the 1933 Clitheroe Co-op Pageant, as embarrassingly revealed by Dennis Tanner in a Street version of 'This is your Life')

RITA & LEN FAIRCLOUGH

Len Fairclough was driving past Bessie Street School one dark February night when his headlights picked up something that took his mind right off the Highway Code. 'The best pair of legs I'd seen since Betty Grable packed up pictures,' he told his pals later.

They belonged to Rita Littlewood. And that was their first encounter. A sort of destiny, for they had a great deal in common. Both had survived tough, unsupervised childhoods; both had an easy-going approach to life and suited their morals to its offerings. Moreover both had explosive tempers if things did not go their way (Rita had not inherited her mother's red hair and wayward temperament for nothing).

Rita's childhood had been spent roaming round the amusement arcades in the centre of Manchester. Her dreams were of showbusiness and she'd somehow struggled into its less spotlit areas via talent competitions and gatecrashed auditions. She got by singing and dancing wherever a club had a vacancy.

Len's tough formative years were spent in the rough end of Liverpool. He was streetwise and a tearaway and his capacity for hard work was matched by his thirst for hard drink.

Neither had been exactly lucky in love. Len's marriage to Nellie Briggs had quickly soured. It was soon all over bar the shouting and his son, Stanley, never forgave him to his dying day for his treatment of Nellie.

Len and Rita – love and marriage?

By the time he met up with Rita, both had been through the emotional mill. Nellie had already departed with Stanley and the insurance salesman, and Rita was having a lean time living as 'Mrs Bates' with a rough motorway construction worker and passing herself off as the mother of his two children.

The up-and-down switchback of their affair ran its course for several years: attraction, affection, fights, farewells, reconciliations. Len had always been attracted to Elsie (he'd proposed several times) and maybe he found an echo of her flame-haired glamour in Rita.

Not until 1977 were all their emotional entanglements sufficiently cleared for them to walk the path to the altar. And even then it was no happy-ever-after story ending. Rita was to storm off, this time to Blackpool, after a row about home improvements and the old marry-go-round was in motion once again.

To give them the security of family life Rita desperately wanted to adopt a child. They fostered two. And when they moved into the brand new home Len had built at Number Seven, it seemed they were at last on an even keel.

Then came the Ogdens' ill-omened Ruby Wedding celebrations. Rita was to sing 'Stardust' to get the party going, when news came that Len had been killed in a car smash – and the secret of his final illicit fling gradually came out.

Rita's broad back had to take one more of life's bad jokes.

More than a touch of Rita Hayworth!

LEONARD FRANKLAND FAIRCLOUGH

BORN: 5th November, 1924 in Liverpool
PARENTS: Ned Fairclough and Grace Frankland. (Both killed in wartime bombing.) Father an engine lathe operator.
HOMES: Hunts Cross, Fazackerley, Toxteth, Weatherfield, Bootle
WAR SERVICE: Leading seaman on destroyers, 1943-1945
MARRIED: Nellie Briggs, 12th July, 1949 (divorced, 1963); Rita Littlewood, 20th April, 1977
SON: Stanley, born 8th June, 1950, Mawdesley Street, Weatherfield
JOBS: Apprentice bricklayer and joiner with Hunt Bros., Liverpool (1938-1943). Resumed work with company after the war. Moved to Weatherfield branch 1949. Moved to Birwistles 1962. Then from there to Roscoe and Pitts and finally set up his own business.
DIED: 7th December, 1983

RITA FAIRCLOUGH (née Littlewood)

BORN: 25th February, 1932
PARENTS: Harold and Amy Littlewood. Father, joiner (retired). Mother deceased
HOME: Manchester
MARRIED: Leonard Frankland Fairclough, 20th April, 1977
JOBS: Woolworth's Store on leaving school at fifteen; nightclub entertainer and hostess. Manageress and co-owner of the Kabin 1973
WIDOWED: 7th December, 1983

Elsie, the eternal Romantic.

ELSIE TANNER

Elsie Grimshawe had been shocking Weatherfield ever since she became aware that there was life beyond the end of Gas Street. It was no surprise to Ena Sharples when this young tearaway 'got herself pregnant'. She was just 16.

Arnold Tanner, the father, 'did the decent thing' and they were married. But for this trick of fate, Elsie would never have stayed on in those grim backstreets.

As things turned out, it was Arnold who disappeared into the big wide world. Three months after their wedding he joined the Merchant Navy, but Manchester was a wartime hive of servicemen in search of honey and Elsie's life was never dull.

Meanwhile, baby Linda was no stranger to babysitters; Elsie's maternal instincts were never her strongest virtue. But when, in 1941, Arnold returned home for two months, she soon had son Dennis to remember him by.

By now the Yanks had arrived and Elsie did her best to make every one of them feel at home. According to Ena there was not an American Serviceman in the North West who did not know the path to Elsie's door.

Yet it was impossible not to admire Elsie. Nothing could crush that big, warm heart for long; no setback could quench her sense of fun and fairness. She never pretended to be other than she was and hypocrisy was foreign to her nature.

Money was never plentiful; her choice of jobs being as capricious as her men – and she was ever the soft touch. When Arnold turned up in 1961 demanding a divorce it was his girlfriend's pleas which pursuaded her to give way.

Elsie was to marry twice again. First to American M/Sgt. Steve Tanner, an old flame from her wartime past. Then to Alan Howard, for whom she temporarily escaped from Weatherfield.

Neither lasted. With Steve she soon realised that she had married a dream. The marriage was over long before he was murdered by a brother officer. With Alan, too, the days of carefree roving quickly palled.

Among her conquests meantime were Len Fairclough, Florrie Lindley's husband Norman, a homicidal art master (for whom she modelled) and Dave Smith the local bookie.

However it was Bill Gregory, the man who once broke her heart by not telling her he was married, who at last persuaded her to sell up and chase her rainbows once more.

Whether or not their voyage takes her into calmer waters only time will tell.

Above: Elsie and Alan – worried about his drinking.

Left: Elsie has news for Betty Turpin!

ELSIE TANNER (née Grimshawe)
BORN: 5th March, 1923
PARENTS: Arthur and Alice Grimshawe of Gas Street, Weatherfield
EDUCATED: Bessie Street Schools
MARRIED: 1. Arnold Tanner (4th October 1939). Div. 2. M/Sgt Steve Tanner (4th September 1967). Widowed. 3. Alan Howard (22nd July 1970). Div.
CHILDREN: Linda (8th January 1940) and Dennis (1st April 1942)

MAGIC MOMENTS OF THE 70's

□ Like many quiet men, Jerry Booth was prey to the occasional magnificent obsession. In 1972, fired by visions of a life on the open waves, he laboured long and lovingly over the construction of an 11′ by 3′ Heron Sailing Dinghy. Len Fairclough's backyard was transformed into Coronation Street's very own Clydeside, and as the craft took shape, yachting fever ran rife. Everyone came to view and embibe the nautical spirit. Jerry, with this unsuspected touch of romantic wanderlust, named the boat 'Shangri La', and competition was fierce for

the honour of crewing it on its maiden voyage. Eventually Stan and Ray, with Jerry at the helm, took to the water. Literally. The thing sank like a stone.

□ On the 11th of January 1978, Ernest Bishop (Stephen Hancock) was in his office at the factory when two young thugs burst in and confronted him. Ernest, a mild and gentle man strong on principle, stood up to them, confident that he

could foil their attempted wages snatch by keeping a cool head – and keeping them talking. The sawn-off shotgun one of them carried seemed like a prop from some bad gangster movie he'd seen on TV. Until the trigger finger tightened and the gun emptied the lead contents of its short, black barrel into Ernest at point black range. He stood no chance. The mindless violence rampant among a workless and increasingly disenfranchised generation had claimed one more innocent victim.

□ The Street's Bank Holiday Party in June 1976 was considerably livened by an impromptu entertainment spectacle provided, inevitably, by Stanley Ogden. For a fiver (but of course) Stan offered to copy the amazing act performed by his old Army chum, Wally, Escapologist Extraordinaire. Stan was duly shackled with Wally's trick chains, and the padlocks securely fastened. Stanley flexed his muscles magically to re-

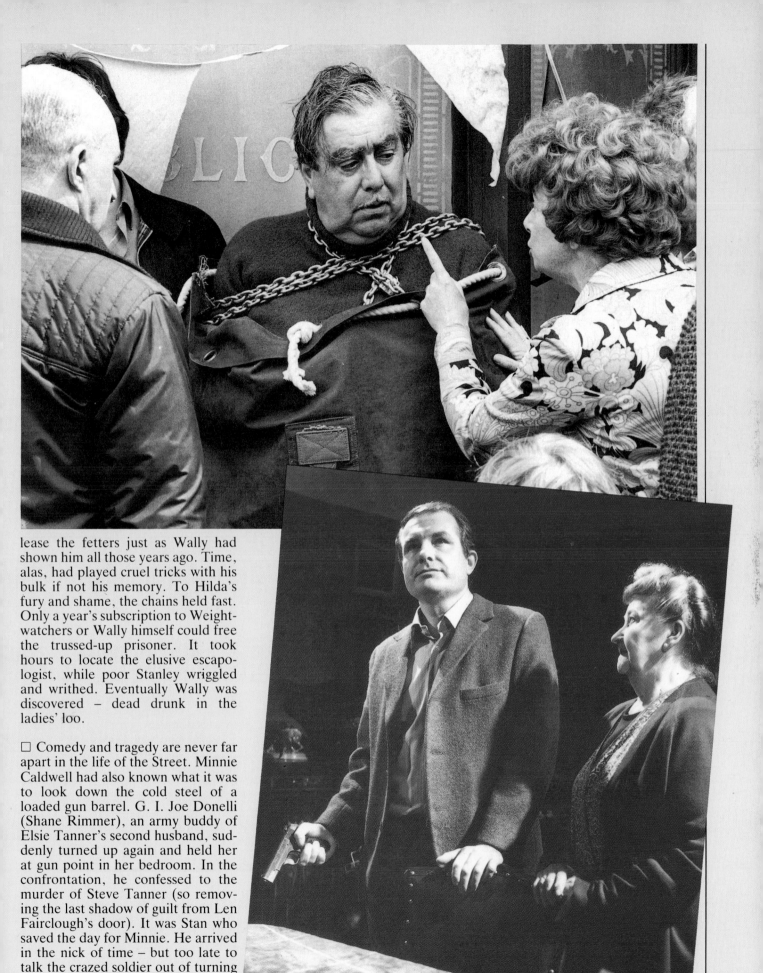

lease the fetters just as Wally had shown him all those years ago. Time, alas, had played cruel tricks with his bulk if not his memory. To Hilda's fury and shame, the chains held fast. Only a year's subscription to Weight-watchers or Wally himself could free the trussed-up prisoner. It took hours to locate the elusive escapo-logist, while poor Stanley wriggled and writhed. Eventually Wally was discovered – dead drunk in the ladies' loo.

☐ Comedy and tragedy are never far apart in the life of the Street. Minnie Caldwell had also known what it was to look down the cold steel of a loaded gun barrel. G. I. Joe Donelli (Shane Rimmer), an army buddy of Elsie Tanner's second husband, sud-denly turned up again and held her at gun point in her bedroom. In the confrontation, he confessed to the murder of Steve Tanner (so remov-ing the last shadow of guilt from Len Fairclough's door). It was Stan who saved the day for Minnie. He arrived in the nick of time – but too late to talk the crazed soldier out of turning the gun on himself.

☐ Ken Barlow's twin son Peter (Joseph McKenna) turned up on a trip from his grandparents' home in Glasgow in the August of 1977. And Ken, being Ken, decides that fatherhood is a serious business. There is a great deal for man and boy to catch up on and Ken feels the bonds of friendship will best be forged by outdoor adventure. So together they set off on a hike in the Peak District; father and son together under the open skies. Not for long, however. Ken rather dents the image of the strong, dependable father-figure by falling down the crags and severely damaging his ankle. Fortunately Peter is a quick-thinking and self-reliant lad in his own right. He summoned the mountain rescue service. And Ken's return to the bosom of Mother Nature ended in a spectacular helicopter air-lift to the nearest hospital.

☐ 'Britain Through the Ages' was the theme for Coronation Street's decorated float in the Jubilee celebrations of June 1977. It would have caused a patriotic sensation – if Stan hadn't flattened the batteries on the brewery lorry used to convey the assembled might of Britain's historical greatness. There was Annie as the Virgin Queen Elizabeth I, Ena embodying all the majesty of an unusually amused Victoria, Fred Gee as Sir Francis Drake, Ernest Bishop as Raleigh, Bet resplendent as Britannia, Ken (rather incongruously in view of his hiking débâcle in the Peak District) as Sir Edmund Hillary the Conquerer of Everest – and Albert as a disgruntled Sherpa Tensing. The gracious smiles were soon wiped off their faces, however, when they had to climb down from their improvised pedestals and foot it to the park to join the Carnival procession.

☐ Near tragedy smashed into the side of the Rover's when the driver of a passing lorry had a heart attack at the wheel and the vehicle careered out of control into the crowded bar. Alf Roberts is severely hurt, but it is Deirdre Langton who suffers most. She has left baby Tracy in her pram outside and there is no sign of her in all the debris. Unknown to anyone, however, Tracy has been snatched by a girl (played by Yvonne Nicholson) Deirdre befriended during her confinement, whose illegitimate baby had been adopted. Deirdre is driven to the brink of suicide by these double shocks, one following the other, and disappears herself. As the police locate baby Tracy, Deirdre is found on the canal bank and eventually calmed into believing that Tracy really has been returned unharmed. It was a hair-raising sequence of near misses.

The 80's

Many new faces had been introduced to the Street's loyal viewers as the original inhabitants dwindled away to one – Ken Barlow. But as the Street prepared to celebrate its Silver Anniversary, the seemingly irreplaceable favourites like Elsie, Ena, Annie, Jack and Albert had given way to other favourites, Bet, Mavis, Hilda, Rita, Curly and the boys.

The cast of *Coronation Street* with Peter Tonkinson who was a storyline writer from 1972 to 1985.

The 80's arrived and the winds of change fairly whistled through Coronation Street with all the ferocity of a Force Nine Gale. As never before was the truth tested in Harry Kershaw's casual assertion, long ago: 'There are no stars in Coronation Street.'

Death, old age or the time-honoured 'circumstances beyond our control' decimated the citizenry of Weatherfield as the new decade got into its stride. Margot Bryant had already retired into a nursing home, forcing Minnie Caldwell to beat a hasty retreat from the district to become companion to a long lost friend.

Doris Speed's age, a closely guarded secret known only to a few friends, family and the Street's loyal Press Officer, Leita Donn (a devoted watchdog and a fan), was made public when she was taken seriously ill. Her legions of admirers were amazed to discover that Weatherfield's indestructible landlady was in fact an increasingly frail old lady, as old as the century.

Violet Carson died after removing herself from the Street for so long. But as Ena's spirit had been kept alive without her presence so successfully, no one had the heart to send her to the great Mission Hall in the sky, and Ena languished in remote St Annes long after the coach parties had ceased to pull up outside Miss Carson's old home.

Jack Howarth, only two years younger than the octogenarian Albert Tatlock, also passed on and the Street mourned another original stalwart on both counts.

Bernard Youens, that most accomplished of comedy actors, had suffered a series of distressing strokes and, until his death in August 1984, Stan's role had to be carefully conceived to accommodate his incapacity. For a time he was immobilized in bed with the celebrated big toe injury and its resulting claim for compensation from the Council. This kept Stanley's backsliding character beautifully in focus without putting the ailing actor through too much physical strain.

Jean Alexander, of course, continued to inject their scenes with all their old pace and gusto so that few people outside the studios guessed how this gallant man had to struggle through each episode.

Over the years Oggie had treated

the Street and its viewers to a splendid track record before his course was run. Will anyone forget the scrawny Alsation dog he bought with Eddie Yeats in order to muscle in on the security game – only to have the animal stolen by the first burglar to come along? Or those hens with which he infested the back yard in order to crack the fresh egg market – only for Ena to discover that Eddie had been supplementing the nests with lion-stamped ones bought from the Corner Shop to encourage them to lay.

His job as a chauffeur lasted exactly one day when his employers discovered he'd taken the family out joyriding in their car. The waste-paper collections he'd begun with Charlie Moffitt and Albert Tatlock netted them each only £3, thanks to Hilda's intervention.

His careers as an ice-cream vendor, home brew beer manufacturer, antique dealer, purveyor of fine fabrics, window-cleaner and night watchman all hit the dust in spectacular disaster. When Len offered to find him work in his building firm,

Gail Tilsley with her
baby Nikky (Warren Jackson).

Tea with Stan and Hilda – some things never change.

Betty Turpin.

Stan put his back out with his first day's labours – and returned with a doctor's note certifying that he was fit for 'light work only'.

And when he managed to sell as his own a song Ena had written, he had the cheek to come back and ask her for another. She obliged – and gave him the tune of 'Onward Christian Soldiers'!

Coronation Street will not see Oggie's like again.

Yet Harry Kershaw continues to be philosophical. 'Sometimes when a bunch of the old ones leave you think: It's the end. The strength's gone. But the Street's like a good regiment. Other characters come through and on it goes.'

Indeed new blood has been poured in by the bucketful during the first half of this decade. Brian and Gail Tilsley have provided the new infant interest with the birth of their son Nikky. Bet Lynch has stepped up to fill the breach left by Annie at the Rover's.

And when story line writers like Peter Tonkinson come to look back over their long years association with the Street and its residents, the smiles on the celebratory photographs seem as broad and spontaneous as before. The only way anyone would know the traumas going on behind the scenes in the Street is by reading the yards of newsprint devoted to the real-life comings and – more particularly – goings of its participants.

Only four of Bill Podmore's regular new writers have stayed the course over the past ten years. It is not difficult to see why. The series is a voracious devourer of stories, dialogue, jokes and characters. No sooner is a new family installed and made to feel at home than some fresh unlooked for calamity robs them of one or more of its members.

The Tilsley's looked all set to become a long-serving clan. They had slipped virtually unnoticed into the mainstream of Street life along with Fred Gee and the Duckworths.

Originally Ivy Tilsley had been seen with her friend, the man-hungry Edna Gee, only as part of the factory workforce, occasionally enlivening the bar of the Rover's with their tittle-tattle. On Edna's fateful fortieth birthday (prior to sending her off on the funeral pyre of the warehouse inferno) it was decided to introduce their respective spouses.

So low-key were their husbands' debuts that scarcely anyone today remembers that Bert Tilsley was originally called Jack! And he was played by another actor entirely – Bert Gaunt.

By the time the 80s were underway, however, both men were firmly established and front-line story char-

> ## 'It was of course absolutely right that Bet should be left high and dry in her moment of triumph'

acters – Mr Tilsley having been re-christened as well as re-cast.

But again the fates were against the story writers in both cases. Peter Dudley became a stroke victim. As a person he was well-loved among his colleagues and everyone loyally rallied round to enable him to keep the role going. In order to overcome Peter Dudley's visible disabilities, Bert was plunged into a bout of deep depression brought on, topically enough, by unemployment.

Hoping against hope that physiotherapy and the natural healing process of time itself would pull the actor through, the Tilsley family saga took on the aspects of a dark Russian tragedy, as Ivy battled to cope with her husband's retreat into gloom, her job at the factory, and the ups and downs of Brian's emotive marriage to Gail.

Finally, however, Peter Dudley's death resulted in the inevitable Street bereavement and within months, both Ivy and Hilda were facing a future of widowhood.

Mercifully there is always a sense of continuity in the Street supplied by such stalwarts as Betty Driver who, as Betty Turpin, is as much an

Ivy and Bert Tilsley.

Summer fun and games in the Street.

essential figure behind the bar at the Rover's as the ale pumps themselves – and just as necessary to its sense of reality. A face that is always there.

Yet even the most reliable of standbys can, on occasions, contribute to a crisis. Miss Driver was struck down with flu on the very eve of recording the crucial episode in which Bet Lynch takes over the most famous pub in Britain. Not surprizingly there was considerable consternation, not to say panic. A neat scene had been planned between the former confederates of the old Annie Walker regime.

Where was the continuity? How was Bet going to manage her first day without her right-hand woman?

Late into the night some hasty re-writing was done and next morning some equally hasty re-learning and rehearsing. The episode proved to be one of the finest and the funniest of the Street's latter years.

'It's often the case when you're thrown back on the inspiration of the moment like that, something extra is pulled out of the hat,' says Bill

Podmore proudly. 'It was of course absolutely right that Bet should be left high and dry in her moment of triumph. That has been the pattern of her life. But it would never have occurred to us to have left her without Betty and only a beautiful but totally incompetent barmaid manning the pumps.'

It was becoming vital to assimilate the newcomers as quickly as possible during those long months when it seemed as if some terrible jinx had settled on the Street, and every new edition of the tabloid Press seemed

to carry news of some fresh disaster. Communal events were given top priority to re-enforce the community spirit. If there was no birthday or Jubilee or Royal Wedding to hand, then a tug-of-war between the Rover's and the Flying Horse could easily be arranged to show that everyone was pulling together – as well as keeping alive the running gag about their rivalry with the other pub.

Mavis enjoys a holiday with Victor Pendlebury (Christopher Coll).

Right: Curly Watts.

Above: up to no good!

It was about this time that Fred Gee, alias Fred Feast, abruptly announced his withdrawal from the Street, amid a further flurry of publicity. Peter Adamson had already been written out after a series of top level rows about his published views on the series, and some altogether unfortunate publicity.

But mercifully there were still characters like Mavis around to re-enforce the sense of belonging and familiarity. And thanks to the artistry of Thelma Barlow, she was able to handle larger and larger slices of the comedy and drama served up for her by the writers. Her courtship by two men at the same time, her hike in the Peak District with one of them and her engagement to the other (culminating in her celebrated wedding day débâcle) was all vintage stuff.

So was the follow-up where, without ever having been married in the first place, Mavis found herself the winner of an unwelcome second honeymoon!

'I'm having a lovely time with Mavis,' reported Miss Barlow, as the scripts rolled in.

In many ways the episodes showing poor Mavis at the mercy of the national Press were all written straight from the heart. From its earliest days Coronation Street has shared a love-hate relationship with the popular newspapers. The best laid plans of producers have often been thwarted through leaks to the Press (the Sheila Birtles suicide scandal was only one among the many). The artists, too, have suffered all the invasions of privacy usually reserved for Elizabeth Taylor or Prince Andrew.

When Julie Goodyear married an American businessman, articles appeared pouring out heartfelt confidences written by people she'd never met, let alone confided in.

So, when Sally Waterman, the ambitious young reporter on Ken's give-away news-sheet reneges on her word not to print the story about Mavis's second honeymoon embarrassment and sells it to the rival paper in order to secure a job there, it was the beginning of the Street's delightful revenge on the less gentlemanly gentleman of the Press.

'Reporters . . . They're like spies, aren't they?' bleated Mavis at one point. Certainly the freelance smoothie, oozing sympathy and sex

appeal, then plastering Mavis's innocent remarks all over the national newspapers next day was drawn from many a hard-learned lesson from this breed.

As Mavis, Miss Barlow, it has to be said, played the comedy and the pathos in all this right up to the hilt, at one point driving Rita to remark drily: 'Still, I should have thought that you, Joan Collins and Princess Di would get used to seeing your names in the paper by now!'

Meanwhile, Mr Podmore was still busy assimilating the new talent at his disposal. The advent of Curly

'I'm having a lovely time with Mavis'

Watts (Kevin Kennedy) as the dead-pan young educated dustman was a gift for Bet Lynch's doomed attempt to wrest some of the glory from the Flying Horse by pitting the wits of her regulars against theirs in the Brewery Brains Trust Quiz. It worked a treat, both in giving Curly a natural place in the pecking order with established favourites – and also in continuing the unbroken record of humiliations heaped upon the Rover's by their rivals.

'I'm extremely pleased with the way the new youngsters are fitting in. With Kevin Kennedy, Michael le Vell (Kevin Webster) and Nigel Pivaro (Terry Duckworth) we have a nicely balanced young comedy trio to bring back a bit of the bite Ena, Minnie and Martha used to put into the Rover's conversation,' concedes Podmore.

To find youngsters like these, the casting net is spread through drama schools and local Reps. But with the repertory system drying up, the need to unearth unknown faces for the older range leads the casting directors more and more to the club and cabaret circuits.

Liz Dawn, William Tarney (the Duckworths) and Lynne Perrie (Ivy) were all schooled in this tough, demanding environment, as indeed was Julie Goodyear.

When it came to finding a mild-mannered lodger for Hilda to fill the vacuum left by the departure of Eddie Yeats and the loss of Stanley, they found the perfect candidate among the pub-and-club folk song fraternity. A successful small-time country-and-western singer, an actor revelling in the name of Finetime Fontayne, he brought to the role of Henry Wakefield exactly the right blend of vulnerablity and reserve needed to arouse all Hilda's finer feelings. She took out her curlers in his honour. She poured tea out of her best china. In short, she seemed for once to have a man about the house who appreciated the better things in life.

However the script did not give Finetime such a fine time away from the studios.

When it was revealed that Henry Wakefield was a former blackleg the girls at Baldwin's Casuals went rushing for their rule books to have him sacked. Hilda rose magnificently to his defence in the programme, taking on the whole street when the little man made a bolt for it. 'I think he had more courage, doing what he did, going into work, than all them what condemned him!' she told an open-mouthed Vera Duckworth, rendering her for once totally lost for words.

It was, however, the time when the miners' protracted strike was at its most bitter. Mr Fontayne became the target for some virulent letters and phone calls against Henry's strike-breaking past. This upset him, for he was a passionate socialist and staunch supporter of the miners and their cause.

He was not too sorry when Henry Wakefield said goodbye to the Street and left Bill Podmore and his team searching for another promising newcomer.

This confusion between fact and fiction never fails to fascinate the outsider, though Bill Podmore is by

Hilda's lodger Henry Wakefield.

Father and son – Bill and Kevin Webster.

Two of a kind.

now immune to any surprise at viewing reaction. As we were talking one afternoon he produced a letter from his pocket to prove his point. Annie Walker had just announced her retirement and the letter came from a seemingly sane and rational enough middle-aged couple applying for her job.

'We have had a great deal of experience in the licencing trade and we are sure we would make a suitable landlord and landlady for the Rover's Return,' they informed the shell-proof Executive Producer.

It has gone on since the Street began. When Ena was evicted from the Mission, a kindly widow from Birmingham wrote: 'Dear Ena, I know how alone you can be when you've no place of your own. If you still have nowhere to go, come to me. I will welome you . . .'

The personal assistant to a multi-millionaire based in Monte Carlo wrote to Mr Podmore begging him to find her a similar job, 'somewhere in the world that has Coronation Street on TV.' Bill wrote back after some pause for thought: 'I am prepared to do a straight swap. How are you fixed?'

More humbly a widow put in a plea for Hilda's cleaning job at the abbatoir. 'If Hilda Ogden doesn't take up that offer, I wonder if I could have it?' she wrote. 'The free meat would come in handy as I can't afford much nowadays on my widow's pension.'

Funny or touching as this blind faith in the product may be, it is a sure indication of the utter belief generated in the characters and their adventures. As Tony Warren explained, surrounded by momentoes of his long-ago creation in his small, comfortable flat not far away: 'Coronation Street couldn't possibly be just one Street. Too much has to happen there. But it is an entire community's life condensed into a single street and everything that does happen must be believable.'

WILL SHE WON'T SHE?

The Barlow-Baldwin version of the eternal triangle gave the Street exactly the sort of publicity on which it thrives. A fictional scandal that is treated like the real thing.

Ken's marriage to Deirdre, though not always smooth, was in dire need of a good stir up to stop it setting to the consistency of a bland blancmange in the minds of the viewers.

So, at the Christian Cabaret held in the Community Centre, Deirdre found herself thrown together with Mike Baldwin and all the little dissatisfactions about her life with Ken started to rise to the surface. Ken was taking her for granted. A nice man. A kind man. A good husband. All those things girls count themselves lucky to have . . . But.

By the time Emily Bishop heard Mike Baldwin talking on the phone to Deirdre and put two-and-two together to make a round dozen, the pair of them were hooked. And so was the nation.

The episodes were written with deep human understanding all round. If there were rights and wrongs, as Emily knew there were, there was no real villain. Mike Baldwin was no crude seducer. He merely lent a friendly ear whenever a pretty lady needed to borrow one and trusted to his own confident sex

Fleet Street's favourite love triangle – Deirdre, Ken and Mike.

appeal to do the rest. If there was nothing else he'd simply done a good turn, and no hard feelings.

Nor was Deirdre your typical scarlet woman. She was just a wife who found her life going nowhere rather slowly. She had found a man who offered her understanding and a touch of glamour.

Everything the scriptwriters conspired to bring to the story fuelled the public's imagination. Newspapers ran headlines speculating on Deirdre's walkout and ran opinion polls as to whether she should. Cartoons appeared everywhere. Comics worked Ken and Deirdre gags into their routines.

Sympathy for Ken was hotted up when it was revealed that he'd lost the promotion he'd applied for becaue of lack of drive and initiative – the very qualities his rival possessed in abundance. Interestingly, it was

68

overwhelmingly the women who wrote in urging Deirdre to throw caution to the wind and grab happiness and the good life when it presented itself to her, and the men who loyally backed the cuckold Ken. Something in their situation had touched a raw nerve out there. People cared.

While it lasted, it was one of the greatest cliffhangers the Street had ever known. And just when it seemed that the last ounce of public controversy had been squeezed out of the situation, Ken and Mike satisfied everyone's fevered expectations by engaging in a manly tussle over their lady love on the doorstep of the marital home.

It was Ken who asserted himself, lashed out at Mike and brought Deirdre face to face with the consequences of

"Bloody shame about Deirdre!"

Try a pint, Ken. It just might work.

The showdown; drama on the doorstep – everyone got involved!

her actions with a few home truths.

The suspense was drawn out a little longer as Deirdre went to follow Mike and an uncertain future – but then turned back and faced up to all the things she'd been running away from. She and Ken sat down to sort out their lives. And such was the quality of the writing and the acting that there was never any hint of an anti-climax in this solution. Just an adult acceptance of reality.

69

EXITS FROM WEATHERFIELD

As the Street is played, you win some and you lose some. While Ken, Deirdre and Mike were busy boosting the ratings, others were planning on long-term removals.

Eddie Yeats had bumbled his way into the hearts of the faithful viewers with yet another of the Street's unlikely introductions. As an ex cell mate of Jed Stone he had found a temporary haven at Minnie Caldwell's. In fact this was just one of the writer's many devices to rouse the displaced Ena to fury: *she* had elected to become Minnie's guest and was not at all pleased to find ex gaolbirds in residence.

His face fitted, however. Just the lodger to fill up the Ogdens' spare room now that Irma was off their hands. And so began one of those inspired collaborations which so often happens purely by chance.

Actor Geoffrey Hughes had exactly the magic ingredient to bring an extra spice into Jean Alexander and Bernard Youens' verbal battles. In fact, as written and played, Eddie could have been Stanley's natural son and heir.

Yet, after enjoying some good years and hilarious moments in the Street, Geoffrey Hughes felt his career was being limited; that he was looked on less as an actor and more as Eddie Yeats as the years went by. He did not envisage growing old in the service of Coronation Street.

The writers dreamed up a natural story line to take him away without destroying his credibility or burning his boats if ever he wanted to return. A wedding – shotgun, of course – was written into ´the plot giving Eddie plenty of scope to lose their savings and generally live down to his raffish charms before eventually taking his bride Marion Willis (Veronica Doran) off to a new life.

For Elsie Tanner's departure Eric Rosser's elephantine memory and filing system came up trumps.

Right: Marion Willis.
Below: Renée Roberts with Eddie Yeats.

Pat Phoenix had decided to call it a day and return to the stage. But something special had to lure Elsie away from her home. And Mr Rosser found it.

Back in the dim, dark days of the Equity strike, you may remember, Elsie was locked in an ill-starred romance with Bill Gregory (Jack Watson). He was married and Miss Phoenix played a memorable scene in the Rover's when his wife turned up. It was Elsie at her most courageous and most vulnerable. She let him go without a look.

So, almost twenty years on, Bill Gregory was resurrected from his successful bar in Portugal and off into the sunset went Elsie on yet another sentimental journey.

Above: Elsie alone again . . . Fred Gee with Kath Godwin (Lori Wells Keefe)

Fred Feast's going was not quite so smoothly managed. When an actor does not wish to renew his contract with Granada, he or she will often give the scriptwriters a few weeks' time over and above their contractual obligations to round off the story line conceived several weeks ahead. But Mr Feast stuck to the letter of his contract and Fred Gee's disappearance from behind the Rover's bar was as abrupt as his manner often was.

With the loss of the last Tanner, Number Eleven was briefly occupied by widower Bill Webster and his family. Again, just the sort of new faces the Street needed, it seemed. But Peter Armitage never settled in the role of Bill and yet another wedding drama was played out in order to supply a smooth exit. Bill left taking his daughter. But son Kevin (Michael le Vell) had made a considerable impact both with the viewers and in the plots. He stayed on.

Bill Webster with his daughter.

BET LYNCH

'From Annie Walker to Bet Lynch – is that progress would you say?' sighed Emily Bishop with a sad shake of her squeaky-clean hairdo. The date was 4th February, 1985 and down Coronation Street strode a woman with very different views on progress.

Dolled up to the nines, all signs of last night's celebration hangover bravely obliterated beneath her lavish clown's make-up, Bet Lynch marched the short distance from the Corner Shop to the Rover's Return like a Queen taking rightful possession of her realm. A frilly brolly, unfurled and held aloft as if it were a banner, kept the drizzle off her lacquered crowning glory.

No one was going to rain on this lady's parade.

She paused to read the new sign over the old familiar pub door. 'Like the song says,' she told herself at the sight of her own name up there in green and white, 'this is the age of Elizabeth Theresa Lynch.'

The impossible was happening. Bet, the nation's most enduring barmaid, the woman life had had typecast as the eternal mistress, was at last mistress of all she surveyed. For the moment, anyway.

It had been a long hard slog, that small step from her temporary lodgings at Alf's shop to the dawn of her new existence as licencee of the Rover's. The wartime baby who was born at 15 Clegg Street on 4th August, 1940 seemed to have the loser's number pinned on with her first nappy. At least where men were concerned. Her father cleared off when she was only six months old and no male she ever cared for since then had stuck by her for long.

Even her own son, born illegitimately soon after she'd left Bessie Street School at the age of fifteen, was taken away and adopted by the time he was six weeks old.

No doubt psycho-analysts could tell you a lot about why Bet dresses and acts as she does. Loud and brassy as a dinner-gong in a Blackpool boarding house on the outside, all melting candyfloss within, she first surfaced back in 1966 as just one of the girls in the old raincoat factory. It took four yeas before Billy Walker noticed her obvious charms

Left: Bet Lynch, proprietress of the Rovers Return.
Right: Queen of all she surveys . . .

and invited her to leave her new job as manageress of the local launderette and become the barmaid at the Rover's. Needless to say, Annie was away and Billy intended to play.

Despite resolutely keeping Billy at arm's length, however, Bet soon found she had left the dry cleaning business only to have her own dirty linen regularly washed in public across that famous bar, all too often under Annie's disapproving nose. Early on, she was kicked out of Irma's flat for nocturnal adventures with a lorry driver; she endured the shame of discovering that this same man was responsible for snatching

Brewery bosses Gordon Lewis (David Dacre) and Sarah Ridley (Carol Nimmons) with Bet.

the betting shop takings from Lucille. Naturally, it was Bet who pleaded for him, then sent him on his way.

It was always the same old story: whenever she lets her defences down, life throws dirt in her face. Mike Baldwin dumped her. So did the local football hero she hoped to marry. A love-crossed she-cat Elsie Tanner confronted her in front of all the regulars at the Rover's. An equally infuriated Vera Duckworth entertained them at her expense by dumping all Jack's clothes in front of her heaving cleavage.

But Bet outfaced them all and survived. That is her nature and her abiding appeal. Her defence against a hostile world is painted on her face and poured into her ample frame. The quick wit, honed over many a stony encounter, is a match for the best of them.

However, it did not take long for even this long overdue triumph to turn to ashes. Hardly was she through the doors of her new domain than she was once more the favourite Aunt Sally in the fairground. No staff on duty; a blindingly attractive, utterly incompetent temporary barmaid to supplant her as the main attraction.

'Not much use being t'chief when there's no Indians, it is?' crowed a delighted Hilda.

Bet had learned all over again that as one door opens another slams in your face. Only the name above that door had changed.

MAGIC MOMENTS OF THE 80's

☐ Mavis Riley's dormant maternal instincts were roused when her pet budgie laid an egg. The event was all the more in the nature of an immaculate conception because Mavis had, until that moment, firmly believed her beloved feathered friend to be all male. A hasty re-christening put that little confusion to rights and Mavis set about preparing for the flutter of tiny wings around the flat above the Kabin. She even converted her bra into an incubation cubical and nervously awaited the happy hatching. It was not to be . . . But it took a man from the R.S.P.C.A. itself to convince her that the egg was infertile.

☐ Fred Gee's wooing of Bet Lynch, never too subtle, took another nose-dive when he invited her for a romantic Bank Holiday outing to the park in his car. Bet, who wouldn't trust Fred's hands to stay on the steering wheel any further than she could throw a grand piano, insisted that Betty Turpin accompany them.

Naturally Fred had no plans for a chaperone, but could hardly withdraw his invitation. So off they set. Nothing went swimmingly except the car! Never a gentleman when thwarted, Fred's temper was racing faster than the engine by the time they stopped for a snack by the lake.

And his ferocious banging of the boot lid propelled the car, with both ladies inside it, into the waters. Fred reluctantly affected a soggy piggy-back rescue, but Bet's revenge was short-lived when her would-be wooer delivered her safely to the bank – only to dump her in a cow pat.

☐ The rivalry between the Rover's and the Flying Horse turned into a battle of wit and intellect when Bet Lynch took up the challenge of a Brains Trust and entered Ken, Curly, Mavis and Percy Sugden to carry her colours. All went well – neck and neck until the final question. It was the hapless Percy who blew the whistle on the Coronation Street chances of glory with a soccer question that looked like an open goal. 'Who scored the hat trick in the 1966 World Cup Final?' Quick as a flash Percy spoke up: 'Bobby Charlton'. It was Geoff Hurst. Once again the Flying Horse left the battlefield with its tail in the air.

□ Old Soldier Albert Tatlock had refused to accompany his old comrade Monty Shawcross to the London Rememberance Day Parade. Albert hated the new-fangled Service, shifted to the nearest convenient Sunday to the signing of the 1918 Armistice. He was, however, heartbroken when he heard that Monty had collapsed and died before the ceremony. He made amends in the only way he knew how; he sold his precious Military Medal for £22 and purchased a wreath. And all alone at the Manchester Cenotaph at the eleventh hour of the eleventh day of the eleventh month paid his own one-man tribute to his fallen comrades – and to Monty. It was a moment to move the bravest heart.

□ Connie Clayton had scarcely had time to move into Number Thirteen and settle in before she was inadvertently embroiled in a full scale Street row with Vera Duckworth. It all began over a dress Vera had designed for herself to go to a dance with Jack. Its frills and flounces, over which the obliging Connie had laboured at her sewing machine, looked dreadful. The fault was entirely Vera's. She'd wanted them and she didn't suit them. But Connie spent the rest of the day putting things right in time for the event. And Vera's gratitude was boundless – until she got the bill. A feud developed to rival the Montagues and Capulets – complete with its own Romeo and Juliet. Caught in the crossfire were Terry Duckworth and Andrea Clayton, though the only poison delivered came from Vera's tongue.

Weddings

8th March 1961	Joan Walker married Gordon Davis.
1st October 1961	Concepta Riley married Harry Hewitt.
20th June 1962	Christine Hardman married Colin Appleby.
1st August 1962	Valerie Tatlock married Kenneth Barlow.
19th October 1963	Myra Dickenson married Jerry Booth.
18th December 1965	Irma Ogden married David Barlow.
4th September 1967	Elsie Tanner married Master Sergeant Steve Tanner.
29th May 1968	Jenny Sutton married Dennis Tanner.
22nd February 1970	Elsie Tanner married Alan Howard.
3rd April 1972	Emily Nugent married Ernest Bishop.
29th October 1973	Janet Reid married Kenneth Barlow.
10th July 1974	Maggie Clegg married Ron Cooke.
7th July 1975	Deirdre Anne Hunt married Raymond Anthony Langton.
20th April 1977	Rita Littlewood married Leonard Frankland Fairclough.
2nd March 1978	Renée Bradshaw married Alfred Sydney Roberts.
28th November 1979	Gail Potter married Brian Tilsley.
11th May 1981	Eunice Nuttall married Frederick Gee.
24th July 1981	Deirdre Langton married Kenneth Barlow.
31st October 1983	Marion Willis married George Edward Yeats.
1st January 1985	Elaine Prior married Bill Webster.
23rd December 1985	Audrey Potter married Alfred Sydney Roberts.
14th May 1986	Susan Barlow married Mike Baldwin.
8th October 1986	Sally Seddon married Kevin Webster.

Jenny Sutton and Dennis Tanner. May '68.

David Barlow and Irma Ogden. Dec. '65.

Ken Barlow with Valerie Tatlock. So young!

Joan Walker on Father Jack's arm. March '61.

Harry Hewitt with Concepta Riley. Oct. '61.

Master Sergeant Steve Tanner
with Elsie Tanner. If only they had known...

Ray Langton with Deidre Hunt. July '75.

Jerry Booth with Myra Dickinson –

how proud of him she looks!

Alf Roberts with Renée Bradshaw. March '78.

Ken and Deidre
will Ken be third time lucky?

Alan Howard with Elsie Tanner —

a very glamorous pair!

Len Fairclough and Rita Littlewood.
April '77.

Emily Nugent and Ernest Bishop – poor Emily

Gail Potter and Brian Tilsley –

young love!

Eddie Yeats with Marion Willis — what a happy pair!

Fred Gee with Eunice Nuttall. May '81

Elaine with Bill Webster — soon to leave us.

NEAR MRS

The Street is famous for its brides and grooms who never were. Emily Bishop started it all back in the 60s by ducking out of her betrothal to Leonard Swindley at the last minute. And practically twenty years later she kept the tradition alive when, on the 10th September, 1980 she happily got hitched to local petshop owner Arnold Swain only to discover, two months later, that he'd omitted to dissolve his first marriage. Emily was a bigamist!

Albert Tatlock's half-hearted attempt at a second marriage to the widow Pickens (Doris Hare) was stopped by divine intervention. The vicar was delayed when his car broke down and Albert used this heaven-sent remission to reconsider his offer. He did not reconsider the honeymoon he'd booked, however, and went off to enjoy it – alone. That was on the 1st September, 1969.

Of course the most celebrated of all the near Mrs who never quite walked up the aisle was Mavis Riley. To the Street's perennial spinster, love like sorrows came not singly but in battalions. Or at least in doubles. Victor and Derek both wooed her; Mavis eventually chose Derek.

The date selected for their nuptials was 26th August, 1984 and Mavis when the day dawned looked a dream. Her pale lilac suit and Princess Di hat transformed her into a picture just waiting for a bridal photographer to snap. But it was Mavis who snapped.

Few who saw that episode will forget how Thelma Barlow ex-

Above: Emily Bishop with Arnold Swain – a lucky miss!

Left: Albert Tatlock with Alice Pickens.

Right: Mavis Riley and inset – Peter Baldwin.

plained Mavis's reasons for not going through with the wedding. It was a liturgy on the meaning of real love. The spray of ostrich feathers in her hat trembling like her voice, Miss Barlow's gifts for combining sentiment and comedy were never better exercised.

Sadly, Mavis's sudden burst of courage was somewhat flattened when she learned that Derek (Peter Baldwin) hadn't turned up either. Two pairs of cold feet had turned away from matrimony's path at the last minute.

Part of Miss Barlow's pleasure in playing those episodes sprang from the fact that she had met Peter Baldwin at her very first job in a repertory company twenty-nine years previously when they were both aspiring juveniles. 'An added bonus, that,' she laughed.

DEATHS

eath's winged chariot rattled over Coronation Street's cobbles before the programme had been on the air a month. May Hardman (Joan Heath) was the first to die. The mother of Christine, she died of a heart attack in her armchair on New Year's Eve 1960, and viewers were given a calm close-up of death's peaceful visage to see them into 1961.

Ida Barlow was the next to succumb. From the outset Noel Dyson had made it perfectly clear that she did not want to sign on for more than nine months. Her home and her husband were in London and so everyone knew that sooner rather than later Ida would have to be written out.

As we have seen there was no way the writers could suddenly turn this devoted wife and mother into a roving adventuress so Harry Kershaw told her, when she was asked how they were going to affect her exit, that she was going to die.

'I'd rather Ida didn't die from anything to do with the heart,' she told him. Harry assured her that he had something more along the lines of a double-decker bus in mind.

'Marvellous!' Miss Dyson exclaimed, happy to know that Ida's fate now lay in the capable hands of the local transport department. Her last bus duly arrived on the 13th

September 1961.

It was, however, back to the cardiac arrests when Martha Longhurst (Lynne Carol) was struck down on 13th May, 1964 in the Snug of the Rover's as part of Tim Aspinall's Great Purge.

The omens for Elsie Tanner's wedding to her American army sergeant Steve Tanner (Paul Maxwell) were ominous indeed when Harry Hewitt was crushed to death repairing Len's van on that very day, 4th September, 1967. Sure enough, only a year later the vultures had replaced the love birds; Steve Tanner lay dead at the bottom of a flight of stairs and Len Fairclough was suspected of murder. A very messy business.

In 1970 came news of David Barlow's death in Australia.

That same year the mystery of Steve Tanner's death was finally wrapped up when an army colleague shot himself at the luckless Minnie Caldwell's house after admitting that he had pushed his buddy down the stairs.

The electrocution of Val Barlow (Anne Reid) came as an enormous blow to millions of viewers. They were used to death among the old or outsiders. But Val was young, in the prime of her life and her popularity. In reality, of course, it was another convenient way of relieving an actress of her obligations while boosting the viewing figures. Val's death was big news next day.

Betty Turpin's husband Cyril, the ex police sergeant died in 1974. And in 1975 Frank Barlow, Edna Gee and Jerry Booth were all featured in the Street's obituary columns. News of Jerry's death was discreetly fitted into the script in deference to the shock of Graham Haberfield's own untimely end.

It was a lean year for the undertakers in 1976, however. Not a single booking.

Mavis Riley's Auntie Edith (Marjorie Sudell) died in 1977 as did Ken's second wife Janet, by her own hand. And in 1978 Ernest Bishop was brutally gunned down in the dramatic wages snatch that left Emily a widow.

Top: May Hardman (Joan Heath).
Left: Ida Barlow (Noel Dyson).

Ena was the stuff on which Coronation Street was built. And with all the new casting, renovations and re-building going on, it was almost like securing the foundations to keep her character alive for as long as possible.

Another great loss to the Street's founding spirit was Albert Tatlock's demise. Only the death of the much loved Jack Howarth could have brought about Albert's disappearance from those cobbled paths. Like Ena, Albert was part of the district's history. Their reminiscences about the old days were a story line in themselves. Wonderful value and supplying exactly the right touch of family feeling and familiarity to bind the programme into the viewers' hearts.

For here, as Tony Warren says, is where this serial scores over all the glossy American imports and over the attempts by other companies to counterfeit its appeal for other regions. Who really cares if *Dynasty*'s Alexis perishes in a blazing barn, or *Dallas*'s J.R. gets shot in his ranch house?

Ena Sharples (Violet Carson).

Val's uncle Albert Tatlock.

Valerie Barlow safe in Ken's arms.

The difficulty of separating fact and fiction is never so accute as in dealing with deaths in the Street, of course. Violet Carson died not long after Ena had left the Street indicating that she 'might not be back'. But somehow the moment did not seem right to bring to a close the old lady's association with the programme.

These are merely glossy celluloid confections. Pure escapism, not to be believed in.

During Jack Howarth's last illness Albert had been represented as staying with his daughter Beattie (Gabrielle Daye) and it was from there that news of his death was relayed to the Street. In many ways it was a replay of the equally invaluable Jack Walker's departure when Arthur Leslie had died suddenly in 1970. To cushion the feeling of loss it seemed better to keep their deaths at

Jack Walker (Arthur Leslie).

one remove from the Street itself. So Jack, too, was staying with his daughter Joan when his time came.

Both these delightful men had spent a lifetime in the theatre before coming to the Street. There was nothing about the business they did not know or understand and people like William Roache still speak with unaffected gratitude about how much they were able to teach the youngsters of the cast back in those early days, just by their example. 'If you were wise you just sat around

Len Fairclough (Peter Adamson).

and watched Jack Howarth go through his lines and you learned more than you could at any drama school,' says Roache.

Success had come to both of them too late for it to turn their heads. Like the true professionals they had been all their lives they simply came to the studios equipped for the job, got on with it and then went home.

Besides Albert, the 80s have already claimed three other major characters. Alf Robert's wife, Renée (Madge Hindle) died in a traffic accident while Alf was teaching her to drive – a salutary lesson, perhaps, to all wives who accept driving lessons from their husbands, for it was in the middle of the inevitable row that the tragedy occurred.

Then followed the uneasy disappearance of Len Fairclough. Peter Adamson's association with Granada had for a time grown rather strained and they were not slow in pointing out that he had broken the

terms of his contract by publishing articles about the Street in the Press. The parting of the ways was made. But Adamson was more than disappointed to know the manner of Len's going. Not just a car smash, but on the way from a tryst with another woman. Peter Adamson said at the time that he felt Len's memory had been served badly by being revealed as a philanderer. But with a tight story-schedule to maintain, Coronation Street cannot afford to forego a touch of drama when it presents itself. Death in a car accident is always a tragic waste of life: in Coronation Street it is also a tragic waste of potential.

However, with the death of Stanley Ogden, his absence was tragedy enough. Bernard Youens had turned Stanley into one of the giants of Street mythology. And this was no light matter. As we know Alan Rothwell happily had David Barlow killed off because he felt that the

Street was dominated by its women-folk.

But with Stan and Hilda the impact was so finely stitched together that no one could see the join. Hilda's quick-witted invective was goaded by Stan's sloth-like approach to life, while Stanley's shifty ways were only multiplied by Hilda's incessant attempts to put some backbone into him.

It was a tragic irony that Bernard Youens' death should finally bring the Royal Television Society to the realization that here in Coronation Street was acting of the highest calibre. They awarded Jean Alexander their own version of Hollywood's

Oscar for her memorable performances in which Hilda bravely faced up to Stanley's death.

Rightly so. They were a model of the actor's art to take their place alongside Dame Peggy Ashcroft, Celia Johnson, Sir Michael Hordern, Alan Bates and the long list of other illustrious winners of this most coveted accolade for the Best Television Performance of the Year. Not one tear too many; not one reaction misjudged. Only when she was closing Stanley's battered old spectacle case did Miss Alexander allow Hilda a private display of her grief. Everyone who had experienced the loss of a loved one knew how the smallest,

should have been for the scenes she played both as a private and a professional tribute to her partner for twenty years.

'Whatever fame I've got, Stan was responsible for a good deal of it. I wrote Hilda's tribute on the wreath myself and in my own words,' she told me shortly after she had recorded those outstanding scenes. 'I knew exactly what she would have wanted to say and I knew exactly how she would behave. I told the scriptwriters; she won't cry in public, you know. I'd seen how my own mother dealt with my father's death and I knew no one would ever see Hilda shed a tear if she could help it. Her pride would not allow her to let Stanley down like that.'

Stanley and Hilda in a rare romantic moment. *Below:* Stanley Ogden.

'Whatever fame I've got, Stan was responsible for it. I wrote Hilda's tribute on the wreath in my own words'

most commonplace object can suddenly bring back an entire relationship. Miss Alexander was murmuring no platitudes when she confessed after her presentation how very sad she was Bernard Youens was not there 'to share this wonderful tribute'.

Had there been justice in such awards the pair would undoubtedly have been honoured years ago together for that marvellous second honeymoon episode in Room 504 with Stanley drunk on free champagne and Hilda high on the five star luxury of her hotel. It was twenty-five minutes of pure comic drama that had it been a 'Play for Today', would undoubtedly have covered its players, its writers, and its director in glittering prizes.

Yet it was fitting that if she were to win television's highest award it

In choosing these two episodes therefore, the Royal Television Society was honouring Bernard Youens' contribution to the partnership and to the series.

Bernard Youens, like Jack Howarth and Arthur Leslie, happened to be in the right place at exactly the right time. And in Jean Alexander and Doris Speed, the right partners were on hand too. Without Coronation Street as like as not they would have died without anyone outside their families and the business acclaiming their work at all. Luck plays as great a portion as talent when it comes to achieving success in the acting profession. Temperament is the other factor needed to sustain that success when it comes.

When their luck came, these men had the talent and the temperament to make their lasting mark. Their deaths and the deaths of their characters were grievous losses.

DISASTERS

Coronation Street has never been short on dramatic incident. But perhaps the most mileage, quite literally, was squeezed out of the residents' trip to Windermere by coach.

The driver taking them had unknowingly picked up the wrong vehicle from his depot. Not until too late was it discovered that the one he had taken by mistake was due for emergency repairs to a faulty track rod.

A call was put through to the police the minute the danger was discovered. But by now the party were half way through their outing and having the sort of innocent (and not so innocent) adventures that are common currency in community high jinks. Ray Langton, as ever, strayed where he should not and a fracas had ensued over that. But what outing is complete without that sort of thing? There had been unscheduled stops for much needed loos. And what coach party hasn't needed those? Only one thing was not in the usual formula. The driver decided on an alternative route home.

By the time the coach was racing through the night on the return journey, almost the entire county police force was out looking for them. When the alarm had been raised at first it had seemed a matter of routine to put a patrol car along their scheduled route and transfer them to their rightful coach for a safe ride home. Only they were not on their scheduled route.

But as time passed, panic mounted. Their predicament was

played out like some Hitchcock thriller. And the crash, when it came, in no way ended the suspense.

On the 29th October, 1969 no one was quite sure if the scriptwriters had gone totally mad and killed off the entire Street. They hadn't, of course.

When help arrived at the shattered wreck, both Jack Walker and Minnie Caldwell lay unconscious, Albert's arm was broken, Maggie Clegg had broken her pelvis, Elsie had pulverized her wrist, Dickie Fleming had dislocated his shoulder, and Val was cut about the head. Ray Langton suffered most. He was paralysed from the waist down for several weeks but recovered the use of his nether regions to continue his old way of life before too long!

Minnie lay unconscious in bed for a long time and Ena, who had suffered nothing more than bruising, steadfastly refused to leave her side until she was well enough to sit up and be told off.

Ena was not nearly so compassionate when a fractured gas main endangered the backs of the entire row and the Street was evacuated to the Mission Hall under Leonard Swindley's kindly if officious protection. Having told him she was visiting a sick aunt, she had sat drinking milk stout while poor Miss Nugent had to make all the arrangements for the evacuees. And when she returned she made it plain that she regarded their plight as an unwarranted invasion of her privacy.

Ena apart, however, it was a valuable look at the way a community like Coronation Street knits itself together under siege conditions. There was a camaraderie not seen since the darkest days of the war. Annie and Elsie (who'd brought her TV – 'What else 'ave I got worth saving?') were suddenly friends as well as neighbours. Young David Barlow was able to prove to the old soldier Albert that he could improvize an alarm system that would have worked even in trench warfare. It was, ruminated Albert fondly, just like this in the Blitz.

Every Blitz must have its Hitler, of course, and Ena stepped into these jackboots unerringly, ordering radios to be turned down, switching off the lights – and getting caught without her teeth in the morning for her pains.

The site where Ellington's Raincoat Factory once stood became a

Above: Coach disaster 1979.

Right: A gas leak fills the Mission.

regular disaster area in the years after its redevelopment. The luxury block of flats that was built in its place was, of course, where Val Barlow met her death through the faulty wiring in a hair dryer. Fire raged through the block and, when the building was inspected to assess

Above: Ena lying in the traincrash rubble.

Below: The set for the traincrash.

Right: A fire which destroyed the Baldwin factory.

the damage, a major structural fault was discovered.

When they, in turn, were razed to the ground and the Warehouse built in their place, the 999 emergency services were soon busy again. This time it was Edna Gee's turn to perish in the blaze. Vandals, from Ken's Community Centre had broken in during the night and left a cigarette smouldering in a mattress. When Edna next day opened the door, thinking to get a little peace and quiet in order to combat the hangover from her birthday celebrations, the place exploded like a fire bomb.

There have been other equally bad moments. A lorry crashed into the side of the Rover's when the driver died at his wheel of a heart attack, and Deirdre went frantic

thinking Tracy was buried in the wreckage.

But the most spectacular of all the calamities to befall this little acre was the night a train ploughed over the viaduct and Ena was trapped in the rubble. The images captured by the cameras spoke for themselves. The mighty locomotive mangled and lifeless emitting clouds of steam, and its human counterpart, Ena, inert and unconscious with all the steam knocked out of her.

Being more armour-plated and resilient than your average train, of course, Ena suffered nothing worse than bruises and shock. So, very likely, did the nurses who had to cope with her in hospital before she discharged herself and turned up one week later in the Snug of the Rover's to order a bottle of her favourite medicine.

90

FLEETING FACES

Well over 2,000 artists have worked at one time or another in front of the cameras on the Coronation Street sets. For some it was a steady job, for others a stepping stone, and occasionally it was a guest appearance. Among those who went on to bigger things was the very young David Jones who appeared briefly in 1961 as Ena's grandson Colin. He found a great deal of fame and no small fortune by changing his name slightly (to Davy), crossing the

Above: Davy Jones later a Monkee.

Left: Chris Sandford.

Atlantic and becoming part of the Monkees – the group American TV assembled as their answer to the Beatles.

Chris Sandford was actually brought into the Street in 1963 as one of Dennis Tanner's long line of entertainment disasters. But the records he made under Dennis's 'management' brought him to the notice of the pop world. Dennis had given him the stage name of Brett Falcon – and as such Chris got two numbers in the charts!

For the late Richard Beckinsale, it was his first TV role. Arresting Ena during her pensioners' sit-in in the guise of young P.C. Willcocks obviously put him off law-and-order roles forever; his television name was made as the young lag in 'Porridge', the Jack-the-Lad of 'Rising Damp', and the eager Lothario of 'Lovers'.

Max Wall, perhaps the greatest of our surviving variety clowns, put in a guest appearance as some unlikely romantic interest for Elsie Tanner. On her trip to Majorca, so the story went, Elsie met the ageing Harry Payne. And in 1978, Mr Wall appeared to prove it.

Len Fairclough's relations with his son Stanley were, to say the least, distant. Which was just as well for the casting department, since the boy they engaged for the part was

Left: Far left – Richard Beckinsale.

Above: Max Wall as Harry Payne, Elsie's ageing beau.

Left: Len Fairclough with his son Stanley (Peter Noone – later Herman of Herman's Hermits).

Below: Dennis Tanner with Charlie Moffitt (Gordon Rollings).

Peter Blair Denis Bernard Noone who, like Davy Jones, trimmed his name and took the short cut to success as Herman with his group the Hermits. At the age of sixteen he was at the top of the pops with his record 'I'm Into Something Good'.

Gordon Rollings enrolled as a regular in 1964. His character, Charlie Moffitt, became the resident comic at the Viaduct Sporting Club. Although his stay in the Street was comparatively brief his impact was enormous. He died in 1985 but his lugubrious features helped sell gallons of ale each night as part of a very successful advertising campaign on TV.

THE SETS

When designer Denis Parkin and the producers of that first episode chose Archie Street as their model for Coronation Street, they did not know the size of the problems they were giving themselves. As streets go, it could not have been more modest nor more ideal for their purpose.

The pub and Corner Shop at each end fulfilled their basic requirements as far as day-to-day commerce and meeting purposes went. The houses with their stumpy square bay fronts and low skylines were just the backdrop they envisaged.

Moreover, far from feeling piqued at being identified as the blueprint

for Granada's new 'kitchen sink' saga, the residents of Archie Street revelled – albeit briefly – in the spotlight's glow.

Their MP, Frank Allaum, took to calling himself 'the member for Coronation Street'. A survey was even published in one of the national papers comparing the real lives of Archie Street's inhabitants with their television counterparts in Coronation Street. And the distinction between the rough paper pattern and the carefully tailored finished article was blurred even further when Archie Street's worn-out homesteads were finally bulldozed flat to make way for highrise flats. 'Is This The End of Coronation Street?' demanded banner headlines.

It was scarcely the start of Coronation Street as a set piece. Particularly as, at that time, so much of the transmissions came live from inside the studios.

Archie Street.

The problems of fitting up these unwieldy Archie Street replicas, even scaled down for the studio to about three quarters of their proper size, was from the outset an endless headache of storage and space.

'When editing techniques liberated us from the restrictions of going out live we decided to search around for a permanent outdoor setting that would meet all the requirements we had devised for ourselves,' recalls Podmore. 'It was a nightmare task.'

The irony was that those apparently endless rows of Coronation Street look-alikes were, like Archie Street itself, fast disappearing beneath, or being dwarfed beside, the 60s craze for skyscraper slum-clearance schemes.

Then someone, no one is quite sure who, looked out from the gleaming glass edifice of Granada's modern headquarters. And there it was. Grape Street!

A row of seven derelict houses sandwiched between a pub and a shop. And at the end of it – a viaduct. Right there in the company's own back yard.

'Who could believe luck like that?' asks Podmore, a man who clearly does believe in just that sort of luck when it comes to the charmed life of his series.

With a little adjustment to the exteriors of this run-down terrace, Coronation Street took on a fresh out-door life. The expense of resetting the cobbles to match up with those Denis Parkin's team had originally painted on the studio floor was thought hardly justified in the cause of realism. But of course the discrepancy was spotted.

'Is this the end of Coronation Street?' demanded banner headlines

This was, however, a small price to pay for the freedom the bricks and mortar of a backlot set gave everyone. Not to mention the amount of studio space it released for the rest of the settings needed in a programme.

With Grape Street on their back

Building the outdoor set and the impressive end result – Coronation Street!

doorstep, the world, or at any rate that bit of it relating to Coronation Street – was their oyster. Trains could smash over the viaduct (and they did); Street jamborees could be staged (and they were); carnival floats could come and go (and they have). With its crumbling back yards and its sagging slates, Grape Street could not have been built in a more convenient spot or to more precise requirements if its Victorian planners had been on the board of Granada TV.

There were, of course, considerable alterations to be done. But it was mostly cosmetic and exterior. The inside of the houses, apart from the glimpses seen through the open doors, were not much use to the artists or crew.

The opposite side of the street, on the other hand, has been altered and replanned several times.

It was, of course, too much to hope that there would be a Gothic style Mission Hall in Grape Street. So eventually, to fit in with the prevailing landscape and a vague idea of changing the feel of the Street itself, the fated luxury flats were simulated in a smart concrete exterior shell.

They were little used. Only the Barlows (and briefly Ena) ever seemed to occupy them. But at least the set lent scope for fire-engines and all the drama of a full-scale fire-fighting operation when the time came to make way for something new.

Inside the studios, the settings are as carefully decorated in every small detail as they always have been from the beginning. Annie Walker's par-

95

lour with its pristine, middle-class pretentions, was meticulously decked out with proud momentoes from her past – photographs of Jack, Billy and Joan – until she made way for Bet's more flamboyant style.

'Downstairs' (though the individual sets are all built on the same floor level) the wallpaper in the bar at the Rover's is chosen with as much care and eye for authenticity as an art dealer making a selection for a client at a Sotheby's sale. The restriction on displaying brand names has long since gone, of course. Audiences now are too sophisticated in the ways of television to imagine that a glimpse of a Haig Whisky bottle upside down in the bar's optic measures is going to send people rushing up to the off-licence for a crate of the stuff.

The Corner Shop, too, is now freed from these silly commercial considerations and can display its wares without any coyness, providing no one comes in complaining bitterly that one brand of washing

Top: Rovers Return. *Above:* Annie Walker's parlour.

Top: Stan and Hilda at home. Above: The Kabin.

powder is not as potent as another, or that a certain kind of bread brings her out in hives.

Originally, the houses were all constructed to have two rooms downstairs and three up. It is assumed that over the years the third bedroom has been turned into a bathroom (though we seldom if ever see one). And in many of the houses – but not yet at Number Thirteen, much to Hilda's chagrin – the parlour and the scullery have been knocked into one open-plan kitchen-cum-living room.

As the occupiers or the fashions change, so do the furnishings. Only Hilda's 'muriel' is forever.

Time moves on here as elsewhere and it must be seen to move on.

By the late 70s the wind and weather (and time itself) were taking their toll. The little street was costing almost as much to patch up and repair than it would to knock down and start from scratch. So it was decided, at long last, to splash out and erect a purpose-built outdoor

setting. And that is exactly what they proceeded to do. Everything that was required was incorporated. It was in many ways a labour of love and faith all round. Love for the fact that in a sense they were re-building history; faith in the fact that it would be needed for a long time to come.

The bricks used were old and grimed from other sites. The mortar was specially constituted to appear old and crumbled yet hold as firm as new. And though the scale was, like most film sets, slightly smaller than

97

Inset and below: The new Baldwins factory.

Baldwin's Casualwear Ltd.

reality, when it was completed you would never know the new Street from the genuine article. Stanley's lilac paint peels off the woodwork at Number Thirteen; Len's posh Georgian-style windows adorn Number Seven.

Inside, all that was required were the props that could again be seen through opened doors. The part of the Rover's bar which leads out into the Street, is fully furnished – the rest is like a compact concrete shelter.

And after Julie Goodyear had

obliged the building workers with some 'topping out' cheer, it only remained for the Street's two loyal fans, the Queen and the Duke of Edinburgh, to declare it officially open.

Oh yes, there was one major adjustment. A narrow side entrance was introduced between the Rover's Return and Number One. Architecturally-minded viewers had for years complained that the Gents in Annie's bar appeared to lead directly into Albert's front room.

Celebrating the new Coronation Street.

VISITS & VISITORS

'There was life before Coronation Street, but it didn't add up to much,' says Russell Harty a founder member of the Hilda Ogden Appreciation Society.

In the earliest days it was not fashionable to go about saying such things. Harry Kershaw tells how he was invariably amused by the number of people who feigned never to watch the programme and then immediately demanded to know if Ena Sharples really had gone shoplifting? Or would Mr Swindley marry Miss Nugent? People who wouldn't blush to watch 'Come Dancing' somehow felt compromised by admitting they tuned in to the Street.

Yet the ratings consistently showed that over half the country did in fact switch on at 7.30 p.m. on Mondays and Wednesdays. Obviously it was the other half.

No matter. The popularity of the programme needed no apologists. It was obvious from their reception at the first Royal Variety Performance that they had taken their place among their peers as an institution in British entertainment. More and more often they were to be seen photographed with royalty, exchanging jokes with politicians, and generally letting it be known that folk from Coronation Street could hold their heads up high in any company.

Violet Carson, as well as being escorted round Buckingham Palace after receiving her O.B.E., was also invited to 10 Downing Street for a meeting with the Prime Minister. It was the time of the Rhodesian crisis and Miss Carson didn't feel she could take up any of Harold Wilson's valuable time; she wrote explaining that an O.B.E. could not compete with UDI just then. A letter came back immediately from Downing Street thanking her for her concern with governmental problems.

Nowadays when the Press ring up Bill Podmore to ask why Ken and

> ## 'It's because they've known Ken Barlow for over twenty years. He's one of the family. You can't expect them to know Prince Charles that well'

Deirdre's wedding attracted more ITV viewers than the Royal Wedding, he can afford to be modest and not lay great claims for his product. 'It's because they've known Ken Barlow for over twenty years. He's one of the family. You can't expect them to know Prince Charles that well.'

From time to time, as producers come and go, the formula for success is varied just a little. When Susi Hush took over for a spell she put the emphasis very much on the female side of the Street. And in order to get its ladies out of what she considered to be a slight rut, she devised a visit that would combine glamour, sea, sunshine and a shot in the arm.

The excuse for all the unaccustomed foreign travel was that the ladies at the Rovers had won a holiday for two in some exclusive Caribbean playground. Bet enveigled the organizers of the competition to re-arrange the bookings and settled for a package trip to Majorca for eight instead. (Competitions loom large in the scriptwriters' array of pegs on which to hang a good situation.)

The minimum of male crew were taken along for the filming. But the footage that came back was certainly different from the usual run of Coronation Street mills. There was never much chance of seeing Bet in a bikini in the back yard of the Rover's. And it's not often you get the chance to catch Emily or Mavis disporting themselves in a one-piece either, though Emily's legs have won many red-blooded admirers on her rare excursions into fishnets for pantomimes.

It was, too, a glorious opportunity to get Rita on the nightclub floor to display all her lusty cabaret training with a burst of Coronation Street style flamenco which left the gypsy dancers standing.

Not all the Street's endeavours are so unashamedly frivolous, of course. It is now accepted among the highest echelons that a single mention of some vital topic in the Street is as effective as a month-long advertising campaign and probably more so. Bill Podmore and Harry Kershaw both hate the heavy plod of do-gooding and incorporate it only when it fits naturally into any given situation.

The Queen visits the Street.

But a call from the Royal Mint asking them to assist in familiarizing the country with the new decimal coinage did not seem an undue demand to make on the ingenuity of the writers. Besides no one else had yet seen any of it. The programme was to be recorded before the coins were in the banks.

A newly-minted 50 pence piece was brought to the studios by an official and handed over. Len Fairclough pushed it across the bar of the Rover's Return, only to have it returned with the words: 'Sorry, we don't take foreign coins here.' It might not have been as enthusiastic a trumpeting of the new coinage as the Mint would have wished but at least it was giving their product a valuable airing.

No one could ever accuse the Royal Mint of payola, however. The official stood by throughout the recording and the moment this brief dialogue was safely in the can, he retrieved his sample piece and left.

Left: Rita takes the floor!
Below: A rare and exotic sight – more legs than the Folies Bergeres!

Other visitors have, however, been more generous. At least in their appreciation of the Street's standing as a national monument.

It would be easy, perhaps, to become blasé under such adulation from on high. But, like most working actors, the cast and their producers know only too well that you're only as good as your last performance and the only way to ensure these continue to pack a punch is to keep your feet firmly on the ground.

The most vivid recollection Harry Kershaw has to offer about that widely publicised trip from Coronation Street to Downing Street – arguably the most two famous street names in the country – is simply that

Above: Coronation Street meets Downing Street.

Below and right: The Queen and the Duke of Edinburgh meet the cast.

they were all dying for a cigarette and Harold Wilson puffed away at his pipe without offering them one.

The coming of the Queen and the Duke of Edinburgh to open the new Street set on a bright sunshiny day in 1983 was, perhaps, one of the most tangible tributes they have received of their solid years of achievement. The Queen and the Duke walked the cobbles of the newly erected edifices questioning the cast and the executives closely on all manner of details.

'I've always said that I've heard

Back to his roots – Cyril
Smith MP.

every possible question that can be asked about Coronation Street and I'd give a gold watch to the first person who thought up a new one,' Tony Warren told me. 'I was so busy looking at the Queen that I didn't notice the man behind her until he asked me the one question I've never ever heard. Before I realized who I was talking to, I said; "Oh, you've just won yourself a gold watch!" I've never seen a Duke look so surprised.'

And what was the question? 'If I told you, everyone else would ask it and I'd get bored with that one too.'

Cyril Smith, Rochdale's Liberal

'Manchester produces what is to me Pickwick Papers. That is to say, Coronation Street'

The Coronation Street cast make merry with a Maori song and dance group.

Dustin Hoffman among the regulars in the Rovers Return.

MP, lived much of his life in a house not unlike those in Coronation Street. He, too, counts himself among its most ardent admirers. 'It is what you would expect from the North. That is, damned good stuff,' he says, putting no fine point on the matter.

When Dustin Hoffman was in town, the first tourist sight he asked to see was the Rover's. In Los Angeles the Street has acquired a cult following, and among the Hollywood cognoscenti, its characters are stars to the stars.

But the most eloquent of the visitors to that small strip of English history was surely the late Poet Laureate, Sir John Betjeman. He was among the Street's most enthusiastic followers. His praises still ring dizzily in Tony Warren's ears. Whenever he has a moment's self-doubt about his creation, he remembers Betjeman's words: 'Manchester produces what is to me *Pickwick Papers*. That is to say, *Coronation Street*. Mondays and Wednesdays, I live for them. I'm very fond of Hilda and her ghastly husband, Stan.

Thank God, half-past seven tonight I'll be in paradise.'

Even for a Poet Laureate that is unequivocal worship.

Sir John Betjeman meets Jean Alexander and Bernard Youens.

JULIE GOODYEAR

From the cradle, many uncanny coincidences link the lives of Julie Goodyear and the character who has spent the past fifteen years electrifying the atmosphere behind the bar of the Rover's. Like Bet's fictional father, Julie's left home while she was still a tiny baby.

For the first five years of her life, she and her mother shared a cramped, cosy Coronation Street lifestyle with her beloved Nan in Heywood, Lancashire. Her surname, so apt for the pneumatic figure she was to develop, in fact belongs to her step-father who from the age of five gave her and her mother the stable family background young Bet Lynch never knew.

Yet, like Bet's son, her Gary was born before she had time to learn what life was all about. Just a month after her eighteenth birthday, in fact. And so naive was the teenage Julie Goodyear that today she still insists it was her mother who had to explain she was actually pregnant. Gary's father was a fanciable, lady-killing draughtsman at the local aircraft factory where she worked straight after leaving school at fifteen.

Unlike Bet's lover, however, he 'did the right thing' and married her. Looking back now she knows it was

Right: Julie Goodyear.

exactly the wrong thing for all concerned. Julie's baby son was left without a backward glance by his father, just like Bet's. Just like baby Julie and baby Bet before them.

Home for the young mother and child was, ironically, the flat above the corner pub her own mum ran. Not a shilling bus ride from the studios where the first pints were being pulled behind the bar of the Rover's.

'Gary was born when the Street was born, in 1960. They grew up together.' There is transparent pride

on both counts. Her son is now a dashing racing driver, proud as punch of his Mum in turn.

'If you ask me honestly what my ambition was in this business, I can tell you that as far back as then it was to be in Coronation Street. As simple as that. The minute I became aware of it I wanted to be part of it.

Her tone tells you that, like Bet, Miss Goodyear is a lady who has come into her own in her own way. And neither got there without a battle and not a few bruises to show for it.'

Above: Bet competes with Annie Walker and Rita Fairclough.

'If you're like Bet you have to be able to take it as well as dish it out. I understand that very well,' she says grimly.

Her first professional set-back, for example, came at the age of six. Utterly convinced of her ability to dazzle, she set off all alone for the bright lights of Rochdale where she had heard that Carroll Levis, radio's Pied Piper of unknown talent, was holding auditions. At a suitable lull in the proceedings she hurled herself at the stage singing her lungs out and dancing like a dervish.

When she paused for breath a large man patted her kindly on the head and gave her sixpence for her busfare home.

Unabashed by the experience, however, she pulled a similar stunt soon after she left school. This time it was the stage of the Bury Palais. She simply grabbed the microphone, yelled One! Two! Three! to the astonished band and began to belt out 'Blue Moon'.

A meat pie hit her smack in the face.

If it was an apt symbol of her life so far, Julie Goodyear had already acquired a highly-developed defence reflex to deflect such rude right-hooks from fate. She simply picked up the pie and ate it – and left to tumultuous applause.

'Of course people do love a loser,' she admits during a break between Thursday afternoon rehearsals. 'But they only love a loser who keeps on fighting. It's not failure that counts against you. It's the failure to get up again afterwards.'

Miss Goodyear is a great advocate for the dust-yourself-off-and-start-all-over-again school of philosophy. To give her son the sort of decent start she had vowed he should have, she once held down three jobs at once.

'But I always knew I wanted to be a performer – with only a hazy idea of what to perform.'

She began by investing an extravagant £50 in a modelling course at Manchester, 'Principally because when I looked in the mirror then, I saw what Bet Lynch looks like now.' The course was just around the corner from Granada's studios. And the newly groomed Miss Goodyear contrived to be seen around them regularly with walk-on assignments.

It was 1966 before her foot seemed on the first rung of her chosen ladder and a crowd scene in the old raincoat factory finally came her way.

'There was something very special even then about the way the cameras picked her out,' says Executive Producer Bill Podmore. However, special or not, it was another four years before those cameras got the chance to pick her out again.

'I knew I'd done well and frankly I couldn't understand why they didn't use me again. But they didn't. Not until I'd done a super little cameo in one episode of "A Family At War".

'As so often happens in life, what you want most creeps up when you're not expecting it. The producer of that episode, June Howson, was chatting to me afterwards and suddenly, quite calmly told me she was taking over Coronation Street and would I like a contract!

'A contract! I don't know if I took her by the throat or kissed her.'

During the fifteen years since that contract was signed she has seen her salary rise to the star-bracket £750 a week and enjoyed the luxuries that has brought, sharing her good for-

All dressed up . . .

BORN: Heywood, 1942
LIVED: Pickup Street, Heywood
MOVED: To Rochdale when her mother, Alice, re-married and gave her the name Goodyear, her step-father's
MARRIED: Husband No. 1, 1960, aged seventeen. Only son, Gary, born same year. Divorced. Husband No. 2. Divorced. Husband No. 3, 1984.
JOBS: Aircraft factory operator; vacuum cleaner sales; washing machine sales; speedboat sales; evening waitress in club; model; small part actress; assistant stage manager; TV star.

tune with her Mum, Alice, back home in Heywood which she has never left.

'But I can't tell you what it was like when I walked down the Street and looked up at Bet Lynch's name over the pub door for the first time. I felt very inadequate. Very. When I thought of an actress like Doris Speed . . . well, no one can ever step into those shoes. And that is certain-ly not the way I'm playing it. What I am doing is out of tremendous respect and love for that marvellous lady!'

Nor has her private life been a jot less tumultuous. She has come through a farcical second marriage, a nervous breakdown, a damaging court case (not of her own making). And she has survived an operation for cervical cancer.

'I have to say that when they told me I had cancer the very first person I told was Bill Podmore, our producer, because I knew that if it was terminal there would be a hell of a lot of re-writing to be done,' she declares, giving a Bet Lynch bar-room laugh at the memory.

'Actually it was the six weeks I had to take off work which almost killed me! I have the stamina of a cart horse. But what I didn't have at first was the discipline.'

Naturally her private life continues to haunt the headlines. No matter how much she avoids giving interviews or shuns public appearances for anything other than the Christie Hospital where she had her successful operation, a tickertape of contradictory newsprint followed her third marriage to American Richard Skrob – 'a kind, warm and loving' widower by her own definition. Coming after a long on-off engagement to one of the Street's directors, and conducted with the Atlantic between them, her marriage has fuelled endless speculation.

Perhaps only Bet Lynch would understand it. 'She is, after all, my best friend,' says Julie with a wink. 'She has to be. After all, she pays my mortgage.'

WILLIAM ROACHE

William Roache is a man who uses words with the care, precision and adroitness of a good surgeon. In fact he fully expected to become a doctor, like his father and grandfather before him, but side-stepped the issues by becoming a regular officer in the Welsh Fusaliers instead. Yet even after thirty years in the profession the direct, analytical edge to his conversation reminds you of both these earlier aspirations.

So, when he describes Ken Barlow's life as 'a one-man Greek tragedy' he is not indulging in an actor's instinct for exaggeration. He believes it.

He also believes passionately in Ken's qualities and his powers of endurance. And it irks him considerably when the character is underestimated. If you belittle Ken Barlow, you have William Roache to reckon with.

'I regard myself as Ken's caretaker,' he says. 'I see him as an intellectual of the home-grown kind. He's had all these experiences – the loss of both his parents, his brother, nephew, and two wives; he's had many affairs, a third wife who went off for extra-marital adventure and several interesting jobs – so that he's not only clever, but wise. Now I see all these experiences as enriching him, not weighing him down.'

And woe betide the Street scriptwriter who forgets this. Mr Roache has not spent a quarter of a century growing up alongside Ken to sit back and have him treated like the wallpaper in the Rover's Return. Nor is he the sort of man to outlive the rest of that original cast of talented actors merely by turning in what he dismisses as 'a tired hack performance'.

He says, warming quickly to what is clearly a familiar theme. 'Because of his qualities, his loyalties, his fighting for what he thinks is right, he's got the label "Boring".

'He's not. He's changed with his marriages, he's changed with his jobs. He's survived and he's learned.

'But I do not feel he has been well used. He has not become what I would like him to be. So I continue to struggle for his believability and his development as much – if not possibly more – than I ever did.

'This is what keeps you very much alive. If there is injustice done to him I will fight it and fight it toughly. Ken gives me a sense of purpose.'

Those famous scenes of domestic strife with Deirdre were of course meat and drink to William Roache the artist and vigilante caretaker.

'As an actor I have not enjoyed myself so much since they killed off my first wife,' he says heartily.

'All of which might mislead you into imagining that here is a man with the combative reflexes of his military training and the professional detachment of his medical background. Not a bit of it.

He is, both by nature and mature

Left: Ken tempted by Sally Waterman.
Below: A young Ken and Val take advice.

reflection, a non-aggressor. A man who enjoys life by taking it seriously and contemplating its conundrums. And he has arrived at what he describes as 'a harmony of the spirit, the body and the mind.' It is, he firmly believes, the only way to achieve a balanced life.

'I belong to no cult or sect. I simply feel, in a religious sort of way, that if you understand the laws of nature and go along with them, as well as heed what is said by men of conscience, then you are actually more healthy, happy and effective.'

And indeed, Mr Roache seems to be the embodiment of these fine virtues. Professionally, he is still able to play the role of a man ten years his junior. He lives a busy and seemingly idyllic life with his second wife and their children, having together survived the tragic death of a daughter they adored and himself the break-up of his first marriage.

'I am a very fortunate man in that my wife acts more or less as agent, manager and sees to all those endless details to do with personal appearances, of which there are many, particularly at weekends.'

And, during his few hours relaxation, she also acts as his caddy, golf being the one outdoor exercise he still pursues with passion. 'So this means we can share that, too.'

Golf, he claims, is the only sport in the world which allows the amateur to play alongside top professionals. Last year he partnered Sandy Lyle in the Benson & Hedges Pro-Am competition. They won – just as he had partnered the winner the year before.

'I suppose I am highly competitive,' he admits when challenged on the subject. 'But only in the sense that I believe in playing to the best of

William Roache.

one's ability and a by-product of doing that is winning. If you only go out to win as an end in itself you can become a cheat or even a psychopath. I like winning only if it means I've done something well.'

'As an actor I have not enjoyed myself so much since they killed off my first wife'

William Roache came to acting late, having spent two years in the desert leading a troop of Bedouin soldiers who spoke no English and thus left him a great deal of time to ponder the direction of his life.

When he finally decided to become an actor he was typically thorough and resourceful. By the time the call came to audition for Coronation Street's original cast, he had served a three year apprenticeship in Rep, done some interesting work for Granada, and moved on to London. With four films and the lead in a TV play to his credit, he had no thoughts of returning North to work.

'If I'd thought it would run twenty-five years I would probably have run a mile. I was very reluctant to sign on for thirteen weeks when I got the part,' he recalls now. 'But my agent told me it couldn't possibly last any longer. All I can say is, it's been a long thirteen weeks!'

Ken and Deirdre – happy again!

DORIS SPEED

Doris Speed came from a theatrical family. And the minute she set eyes on the role of Annie Walker she knew who to base it on. Auntie Bessie.

It was Auntie Bessie who led all the family charades at Christmas time. And it was Auntie Bessie who elected to produce a tableau depicting *Queen Elizabeth I On Her Deathbed* on one such momentous occasion – with herself as Good Queen Bess, needless to say, and her team grouped dramatically around her in attitudes of stricken grief.

The rest of the family were then invited back into the room and bidden to guess the title of this impressive still-life. Without pause, an uncle who'd clearly enjoyed one port wine and one of Auntie's theatrical tableaux too many, volunteered the answer: 'Cabhorse Down On The Cobbles!'

Thus was born the withering look which was to mark Annie Walker's answers to all such displays of philistinism for almost a quarter of a century. Had it been left to Doris, however, Auntie Bessie's spirit would never have lived on, re-incar-

We are not amused!

nate behind the bar of the Rover's Return.

She was doing a play down in Bristol when the call came to go for an audition to Granada for a part in a new soap opera. She said no.

She said it again, more firmly, when they asked her a second time. 'I was never any good at auditions,' she explained later. But when her agent rang and warned her 'You'll regret it for the rest of your life if you don't go,' she went.

What she didn't know, of course, was that Tony Warren had created the role that was to place her among the immortals of television with Doris Speed very much in mind. They first met when she played his Irish nanny in a radio 'Children's Hour' from Manchester and he'd become an instant fan.

Of course, as Annie, Doris got to show the world that she was no mean Lady Bracknell when she graced one of the Street's amateur theatricals, in true Auntie Bessie fashion.

But back in 1960, Doris had been too long in the business to get over-excited about the prospect of a TV series. She'd first toddled into the spotlight as part of her mother and father's musical comedy duo turn.

Joanna Selby who was born on the same day as the programme – 9 December 1960 – celebrates a joint 18th birthday.

Doris Speed.

semi-detached villa in the suburbs of Manchester, just ten minutes away from the studios. There she lived with her mother until Ada died at the great age of ninety-seven and, for the first time in her life, Doris found herself alone.

Nor did she ever overcome her ingrained training never to spend a penny when a ha'penny would do.

'It's not that I'm mean,' she would explain. 'It's just that I've been conditioned to poverty and also, unlike Annie, I'm a life-long socialist, so it makes my heart ache to see money thrown about needlessly.'

Indeed one personal appearance in London, where she stayed in luxury at the Dorchester, was ruined by a frugal breakfast of boiled egg, orange juice and coffee, for which the bill came to £2.75. 'I'm sure there are people who don't mind spending all that on so little,' she sniffed, 'but I'm not one of them.'

Even now, the studios at Granada still echo to actors' favourite Doris Speed stories.

One young actor who jiggled about erratically as they rehearsed felt the full majesty of Bessie's ghost. 'Are you going to move about like that when the cameras are turning?' enquired Doris sweetly. 'Oh, no, Miss Speed. I thought I was casting a shadow on your face,' the hapless foil replied.

'Young man,' said the Queen of the Rover's, 'the dole queues of Manchester are lined with actors who have cast a shadow on the face of Doris Speed!'

Annie always knew she was a star!

Yet all thoughts of fame and fortune were long since abandoned by the time she arrived at Granada for that fateful audition, with Harry Kershaw sitting in to read Jack's lines. 'I thought I was just going to be another theatrical has-been like my poor old father and mother,' she confessed.

Stardom was almost instantaneous, though far too late for her to break a lifetime's habits. 'When you've been poor all your life, you don't change overnight and live like a Queen,' she often said. And she didn't.

Home continued to be a small

PARENTS: George and Ada Speed (music hall artistes)

BORN: Manchester

CAREER: First stage appearance as a toddler in parent's music hall act. Played The Prince of Rome in *Royal Divorce* aged five. Became family's main wage earner aged fourteen. Took shorthand and typing course and acted in amateur dramatics (basis of Annie's reminiscences). Spotted by BBC and asked to do radio work in Manchester. Met Tony Warren in 'Children's Hour' play. Spent years in good repertory companies starring in such roles as Judith Bliss in Coward's *Hay Fever*. Part of first cast of Coronation Street, 9th December, 1960.

PAT PHOENIX

Pat Phoenix had been reading children's stories for a live radio broadcast at London's Earl's Court and we were trying to make a quick dash for the exit. But quick dashes through thick crowds with Miss Phoenix are as futile as rolling a stone uphill with your nose. You take two paces forward to be swept three paces back by avid autograph hunters.

'It's her,' they cry and crowd in with bits of paper, albums, souvenir programmes. Anything to get her name on it.

> '*I always say that if you can play a big dramatic scene with your suspender belt round your ankles and not get a laugh – then you're an actress!*'

Tony Booth, her long time companion, and I wait patiently on the sidelines. The five-minute walk takes more than thirty-five. Miss Phoenix is a big draw.

It is now almost three years since she put aside the mantle of Elsie Tanner and, at the age of sixty, went back to chance her arm in the cold world of commercial theatre. Yet each summer, wherever she plays on tour or in some thriving holiday resort, the houses are packed and the ovation warm. Last year I caught her and Mr Booth at Eastbourne in a vintage thriller. Before the end of the evening, as Miss Phoenix prepared to mount the staircase to certain death at the hands of the crazed Mr Booth the audience were in such a state of excitement that someone could stand the suspense no longer. 'Don't go up those stairs, Pat!' the woman shrieked.

'I would have been worried if she'd called me Elsie. But it's a great compliment to think that you can have that effect in the theatre as an actress,' she admitted when finally we reached our destination: a quiet tea at the Savoy. 'She obviously was believing everything she was seeing.'

Pat Phoenix has always been a woman who could make heads turn, she has always found that easy. And she admits frankly that when she went for the audition for Florizel Street she was 'very arrogant about it.'

'It's not that I didn't want a job. I just didn't think I was television material. I thought they wanted me for all the wrong reasons. And anyway, I'd just landed a job as an interviewer for Granada's 'People and Places' programme. If I was going to go on telly, I thought that was far more dignified,' she admits.

It had taken her years to lose her native Northern accent and she was determined 'never to play North country again.'

What changed her mind were those first scripts of Tony Warren's. 'I remember thinking how I wished they could be seen beyond the Granada region. They were so original, so funny, so alive. The best thing I'd ever been asked to do.'

Her years as Elsie, brought her all

Elsie and Steve's wedding.

the things she'd dreamed of, slogging around the Reps and hoping for a break in movies. Clothes which she loves, a lovely home in the rolling moorland outside Manchester and the sort of star treatment that has stayed with her. Even in the subdued sophistication of the Savoy, they stop talking to look when she walks by.

'Strangely enough I've never believed in the star system. Either you're a good actress and people will pay to see you or you're not. I've always looked on myself as a working actress. I can say that with some

Pat Phoenix – star of stage and TV screen.
Below: Elsie Tanner gives some hardwon advice to Lucille Hewitt.

Below middle: Elsie with daughter Linda and son-in-law Ivan Cheveski.

confidence too,' she adds exploding into laughter. 'I always say that if you can play a big dramatic scene with your suspender belt round your ankles and not get a laugh – then you're an actress!'

Which is exactly what she did one night in a play rejoicing in the title *Shining Hour* when, as they say, the elastic broke. 'I just stepped out of my knickers like a lady and carried on. They daren't have laughed!'

'It's then all your Rep training comes to the fore. You must ask Bill Kenwright about the night I played *Gaslight* to a sell-out audience in New Zealand with both the leading man and his understudy off with food poisoning. I did practically the entire play on my own. His lines, my lines, stage directions – the lot.'

Since leaving the Street she's also been doing what she nearly did before Elsie Tanner changed her life. Interviewing human interest subjects, this time on Tyne Tees TV. The show has won her an entirely new sort of audience and, like the early days in the Street, it goes out live.

It is easy to see why Miss Phoenix is so successful at this. She is a warm and impulsive person. People respond to her. So much so that during

113

Top: Ladies Night at the Rovers Return.
Right: Down but never out . . .

one interview both she and the interviewee were in tears.

'They said afterwards it was the best television they'd put out in years. But I was wrung out.'

She was also busy preparing for a return to the rigours of a TV series as a seaside landlady in a new Central offering called 'Constant Hot Water'. No wonder she is able to bring something special to the role Tony Warren had conceived and turn Elsie into a sort of maternal sex symbol. 'Actually Elsie was a rotten mother. A stupid mother. And I suppose she was the very first of the anti-heroines, for she was certainly no better than she should be. But she had a big, warm heart.

'She had all the qualities to take her out of that Street and far away, but somehow she always missed the boat.'

I asked what was the main difference the character had made to her life and without a blink she replied:

Pat Phoenix died on the 17th September 1986. This affectionate interview by Jack Tinker took place for the first edition of this book in 1985. The publishers wish it to remain as a tribute to a much-loved actress.

'Being able to eat properly. You could tell all the actors who'd landed parts in Coronation Street in those days. We all put on weight!'

Which is probably why one of her fondest memories of life in the studios was the ritual tea trolley they send round especially for the Street workers, as their tight schedule prohibits any time lingering over a meal. 'Tea, and scones with lashings of cream, honey and jam, every sort of sandwich you can think of,' she drools at the memory. 'It was hell for all on a diet, of course!'

For a lady who has given up a twenty-odd years of security, she appears to be thriving. 'Not bad for a pensioner, am I?' she chuckles. 'And why not. I've got the best relationship I've ever had in my life, I'm doing all the work I want, earning all the money I'll ever need, and I'm enjoying everything I do.'

'Here, have a cake,' she added, thrusting the tiered cake stand at me. 'You choose whichever one you want.'

'Well, it's either the tart or the fruit,' I ventured.

'Now that,' she roared. 'Is the story of all our lives!'

You cannot be serious with Miss Phoenix for too long. Even about food.

THELMA BARLOW

Thelma Barlow.

Thelma Barlow was lying in bed one morning reading the latest advance script. It was Mavis Riley's wedding day episode and suddenly she had the clearest idea how the bride should look.

'I sat down and designed the dress, went out and bought the material, took it to the dressmakers and had it made up. Then I chose that Princess Diana hat.'

White, she insists, was something Mavis would never have worn. Not because of anything indelicate in her blameless past. 'She would just have been too worried what people would say, though in her heart she would love to have floated down the aisle as a virgin bride.'

Miss Barlow is a pretty, positive woman and the chic square-shouldered lilac jacket she wore over matching jodhpur style trousers tucked into elegant high-heeled boots was something else Mavis Riley would be too timid to wear in public.

'Oh I know she seems a bit soggy. But she is a sensible woman and nobody's fool. She's never afraid to act on her principles, even when she's vulnerable.

'I think it was far harder to walk into the Rover's afterwards than it was to decide not to go through with the wedding. But then she has changed over the years – how could she not, working with someone like Rita Fairclough?'

Miss Barlow likes to analyse her roles. Her training in the theatre was mostly in classical based Rep and she is as happy and at home discussing the characters in Chekhov, Strindberg and Shakespeare as she is analysing Mavis in the Street.

Yet it was only after eight years as a secretary in Huddersfield that she decided to take life by the shoulders and give it the shake she sometimes feels like giving Mavis. With only a little professional broadcasting experience to her credit she headed for Joan Littlewood's East End temple of experimental theatre, applied for a job and got it.

'I was green as a cabbage but no, it wasn't a difficult decision. It was like Mavis deciding not to go to the church, just something I had to do if I was going on with my own life.'

The painful break up of her marriage recently is now behind her and if you ask her what Coronation Street has given her as a person she doesn't hesitate for a moment, 'independence' she says.

'I went to see Michael Crawford in *Barnum* the other night and I *longed* to be up there among the trapezes. That's the trouble, I want to do it all. One day, perhaps, I will.' And her eyes shone as she said it.

Mavis with Rita – positive as always!

JOHNNY BRIGGS

ohnny Briggs, like Violet Carson, is another exception who broke the rule of using only artists unfamiliar to the general public.

From his earlier days in the profession this bright, go-ahead Londoner had been an increasingly familiar face in films, on television and on the stage at the London Royal Court, that famous nursery for new exciting tales.

'I suppose I fitted in here, despite being seen about a bit, because I was playing a sort of outsider anyway. Being a Londoner, a factory boss, everyone expected Mike to be a bit flash. It probably added to the image rather than detracted from it,' he reasons.

Like so many before him he came to Manchester as a way of doing some regular, gainful work in between rather more attractive offers.

He'd just completed a film called *Au Pair* and a play at the Royal Court when the call came.

Mike Baldwin keeps a close watch over the figures – here with Elsie Tanner.

Mike Baldwin with Deirdre Barlow – a potentially dangerous combination!

'What does it entail?' he asked his agent warily, uneasy about getting caught up in long-term contracts.

'He said: "Well, you just have an affair with Julie Goodyear for three months." So I said: Yeah, I'll have a look.'

The affair ended, but the character of Mike Baldwin stayed on and Johnny Briggs has never had any cause to regret it.

'I enjoyed it right from the start,' he says. 'I began in TV up here in 1960 – the same time as the Street – doing a series called 'Young Generation' with John Thaw and Judy Cornwell. In that way it was like a re-run of good times. And the scripts were fine, too.'

We were drinking fine port in the spacious flat he has bought just a couple of car parks away from the studios. He has another, for investment, nearby too. And at the weekend he travels down South to the country to be with his wife and three young children and also to get in some golf. He has two more children – a son of twenty-one and a daughter of nineteen from his first marriage.

'And I have got grandchildren,' he adds with pride.

Each year he helps promote the Johnny Briggs Charity Golf Match. 'When you've had five children, like I have, who are all OK, you do get to thinking: There but for the grace of God . . .

> ## *'I like his approach to life, his approach to women. He doesn't start affairs, he lets them come to him'*

'I sometimes feel very guilty. In my life I have been very, very lucky. There are many better actors than me, yet I've never had to be a barman, be a busker or wait on tables to get by like so many have.'

His luck began when his mother saw an advertisement. 'It didn't say anything about singing, but they asked us to and I could. They taught us for one day a week and, being a bit of a show off, I enjoyed every minute of it. They picked out six for free training and teaching till we were eighteen. I was one of them. But out of every penny we earned we had to give them twenty-five percent.

'That's where I started – along with Millie Martin, Tony Newley and Nanette Newman!'

His stage school seldom went short of their twenty-five percent of Master Briggs' earnings. His first professional appearance was as a boy soprano in *La Bohème* at the Cambridge Theatre in 1947, and he went on to be featured in many films before, at the age of eighteen, leaving the school for an engagement that did not pay commission: his national service.

'I suppose I'm a veteran of the Street now. I came in September 1976 and it has gone by in a trice. Yet, I've had other jobs that have lasted a month and have seemed like a year. What do I like about Mike? I like his approach to life, his

Johnny Briggs.

approach to women. He doesn't start affairs, he lets them come to him. If they don't, then he's really not at all bothered. He's a very confident and basically a nice guy.'

Smooth talking Mike shocks Hilda with girl friend Maggie Dunlop (Jill Kernan).

JEAN ALEXANDER

At the Garrick Club, where the élite of the theatrical profession jealously guard their exclusivity (they once famously blackballed Bernard Levin from membership) there is a flourishing Hilda Ogden Appreciation Society. Which, in itself, is no small testimonial to the talent of Miss Jean Alexander. However, to gain any real impression of the achievements of this gifted actress in creating a national institution out of a gossipy back-street char, you have to meet her.

Jean Alexander is a poised, softly-spoken and very private woman; the sort of cultivated Southport lady who would move to the next town rather than live next door to someone like Hilda Ogden. Her hair is carefully styled, her clothes are subtle in classic good taste and her face is soft and still pretty in a wary, unspectacular way. In a crowd she might pass as a successful librarian, which is indeed what she trained to be before becoming 'thoroughly fed up with it' after five years and throwing all her natural caution to the wind by joining the Adelphi Guild Theatre in Macclesfield.

Her voice, the classless, modulated tones from which a five bob-a-fortnight investment in elocution lessons and her years in Rep have removed any trace of her native Liverpool accent, still softens when she speaks of the long, successful partnership with Bernard Youens that transformed her professional life. Bunny, she called him; Bun for short.

'And, yes, I still miss him. More than I can ever say. It's like acting without an arm, playing Hilda without Bun,' she confesses. 'There was something very special, very rare about our partnership right from the start. From the very moment we met I knew I could work well with Bunny.

'We never ever needed to discuss a scene or go over a bit of dialogue together. He would come to rehearsals on Tuesdays with his script word-perfect, just as I always do, and we both knew exactly how we

'There was something very special, very rare about our relationship'

Stanley and Hilda – the marriage with everything – from grit (right) to glamour (below).

were going to play it.'

In those long waits between takes they would pass the time playing Scrabble. The more obscure the words they concocted, the more they both delighted in it.

Yet off the set, away from the studios, they rarely met. Throughout their twenty years Street marriage Bernard Youens and his wife Terry visited the immaculately kept house Jean Alexander owns in Southport only twice, and she went to theirs in Manchester just as infrequently.

'I suppose it may seem odd, but that's how it was. Ours was a perfect working relationship. My admiration for him as an actor was enormous and I think he liked working with me. I can't pretend I knew as little about him as a person because I think I understood as much about Bun as anyone in the cast. More probably. But we respected each other's privacy and I liked that.'

With the games of Scrabble gone, she often shares her dressing room nowadays with the bustling, outgoing Betty Driver. They share a common delight in needlework and

Jean Alexander.

She herself has never married and says very firmly she never expects to now. For her approach to Hilda's widowhood ('Have you noticed how neat she keeps the house now Stan and Eddie aren't there to mess it up?') she draws on the experience of her own mother's grief when her father died.

'I knew Hilda would never let anyone see her cry. She'd keep her

pecker up,' she says.

Alone at home now, she indulges her passion for gardening, her interest in historical books and love of classical music. Occasionally, after doing the weekend shopping in Lord Street, she will pop into one of the salubrious hotels of that most genteel seaside resort for a quick drink with a friend. But she is rarely recognized. For a woman voted the fourth most popular female in Britain, trailing only after the Queen, the Queen Mother and Princess Diana, she keeps the lowest public profile of the entire cast.

It would, in short, be impossible to imagine anyone less like the gregarious, busybodying Hilda than this polite, reserved lady.

'But I admire Hilda absolutely,' she insists. 'She reminds me of one of those unsinkable ducks you float in the bath. No matter how many times she gets pushed under, she'll still bob back for more. There's no holding Hilda down.'

Below: Hilda wins a dinner with Mike in a charity raffle.

'Ours was a perfect working relationship'

team up to make delicate items for charity sales. But the gap left in her life at Granada by Youens' death has clearly not been filled.

She took a long cruise afterwards before signing yet another twelve month contract to play the widow Ogden.

'Of course the Ogdens were written at first as a fat lout and his nagging wife. But both Bunny and I decided to bring something more into their relationship than an Andy Capp couple. Whenever they had a scene together we would play it rather more delicately, letting their real affection for each other show between the lines. That was something else Bun and I arrived at instinctively.'

EILEEN DERBYSHIRE

Stuart Hall, one of the North's popular TV presenters, was making an early start, when up the drive of his home came the new newspaper girl.

'Papers, sir!' she said, thrusting his daily order at him – and fled.

It was Eileen Derbyshire at the height of her TV fame as Emily Bishop.

'He did a triple-double-take,' chuckles Miss Derbyshire, 'But at that time in the morning I just didn't feel up to explaining that my son was on a school trip and might lose his round if someone couldn't stand in for him.'

As you might guess, Eileen Derbyshire comes as something of a surprise for anyone expecting Emily. Initial shyness is all they have in common. Whereas all Emily ever managed in the way of motherhood was the brief fostering of two black children, Miss Derbyshire lives a full and robust family life in a small, secluded community outside the city.

Until son Oliver left for university, she divided her time between the demands of her family, five dogs, two cats, a pair of goldfish, and her

coat, might have passed for the smart wife of a successful businessman – which indeed she is. But both the service we received and the glances she attracted from the rest of the clientele were not those reserved for attractive, well-heeled ladies in town to shop.

'It is my great grief about being recognized that you can't be an observer any more. That is as great a loss to an actor as it is to a writer.'

She married her husband Thomas soon after joining the Street. An April 1st bride, she drove round and round the country lanes by the church just to avoid arriving one second before noon.

'Superstitious, maybe, but I wasn't prepared to have my wedding turned into an April fool's joke,' she smiles.

'My son grew up with the Street. I must say I was rather flattered when he became a fan – until one day he said "Mum, I'm so glad you're in this because if you weren't you'd switch it off and tell us not to watch such rubbish!" Talk about deflation!'

The greatest bonus Coronation

Street has brought, she counts as the ability to combine a successful career with a steady home life.

'My mother's favourite saying was: "Eileen, you can't have the penny and the bun." And I agree all things have to be paid for in life. But sometimes I do feel I have kept the penny and had the bun!'

Eileen Derbyshire.

An all star pantomime! with Emily as Dandini.

Emily with the children she and Ernest fostered.

passions for gardening, old buildings and all matters connected with the theatre and arts – on which she has strong and definite views.

We had tea in Manchester's imposing Midland Hotel and Miss Derbyshire in her glossy dark mink

MICHAEL LE VELL

The Street now has a full contingent of young red-blooded males to spice up its story line. But at one point it looked as if it was about to lose its most potent candidate for the role of teenage heart-throb. Michael Le Vell had arrived as part of the Webster family who moved briefly to Number Eleven. When young Kevin Webster's father and sister left the series, a lot of ingenuity was expended keeping the talented young Mr Le Vell within the confines of Weatherfield.

Michael's good looks and easy charm were just what the producers had been looking for. He'd slipped into acting almost without realizing it. After playing the part of Kes in the school production of the play, his English master thought he might as well audition for the same role when his local Rep in Oldham decided to stage the play.

He got it. And stayed on for the lead in *Joby* as well. Since when a succession of appearances in various Granada TV productions led to his being approached to join the Street.

'It's all happened very quickly. I owe that master a lot,' admits this unassuming twenty-year-old, now the owner of his own flat in the Neaton Heath area of Manchester, plus his first car.

'What I can't wait for is my elder brother to come back from Australia and see what I'm doing. I was only a kid when he left and though I send him cuttings and things, I don't think he can really believe it.'

Michael can, however. The producers had just cast the candidate for his first big screen romance as we talked.

Kevin, Curly and Terry
with Gill, Mandy and Elaine.

VIOLET CARSON

Violet Carson was, in many ways, the odd woman out in that first gigantic talent-spotting session. Granada's canny head of casting, Margaret Morris (who went on to become the first woman producer of Coronation Street, incidentally) and her assistant Josie Scott had decided on a strict policy of using only artists whose names or faces were not well known to the general public.

If this was going to be a gritty, realistic serial about ordinary Street people, they did not intend to be diverted from it by employing instantly recognizable personalities disguised in overalls and head-scarves.

Which would seem to rule out Miss Carson, certainly on the first count. Her name had been associated with broadcasting since before the Second World War. And her voice was one of the best known and loved on British radio.

Manchester born, bred, wed and widowed, it was from her home city that she'd first gone on the air in 1935. Her singing voice was rich and full and she used it to cover the entire range of popular music from Italian grand opera to the broad comic dialect songs of her native Lancashire.

During the war, too, she had been one of those tireless artists who spared themselves nothing travelling up and down the country putting on entertainments for the Forces. An entire generation of servicemen remembered with affection – and would no doubt recognize – Miss Carson whatever her costume.

So, when she spoke, would several generations of school children. 'Children's Hour' was one of the BBC's most sacred slots at one time. And between the hours of five and six o'clock each week night 'Auntie Vi' was more often than not to be found there singing, or playing the piano, or acting in a play, or telling a story. Her versatility was her passport to constant employment almost from the moment she had first exercised her formidable tonsils in front of that microphone in Manchester.

Still more folk-fame had come her way as part of Wilfred Pickles' huge-ly popular radio quiz game 'Have a Go'. She was a name all right.

The fact that both Granada and Miss Carson found a sudden need for each other at one and the same time was a happy coincidence for both.

'I felt that I was being very under-valued at the BBC. I had given them most of my lifetime, one way and another and I don't think they could say I ever sold them short,' she once said, years later, when pondering on this sudden change in her fate. 'They could be very, how shall we say, mean with the pennies.'

The call from Granada came just at that moment of disillusion and dissatisfaction. On such chances are legends made. For Granada, too, were desperate. The part of Ena, as Harry Kershaw has told, was about to be dropped as not one of the actresses who auditioned fitted their preconception of a small little shrew-like woman.

'Perhaps if Jean Alexander had been put up for the part we'd have jumped at her in an instant. Many of the qualities she later brought to Hilda were exactly what everyone was looking for in Ena,' Tony Warren admits today. But Miss Alexander did not audition. And so Mr Warren remembered the imposing

Violet Carson – Blackpool's greatest star.

lady he'd once innocently upset years ago in a Manchester studio.

'Granada were not mean with their offer,' reported Miss Carson later, though she was less impressed with the part. 'Compared to what I had been earning as a leading artist with the BBC, the five weeks contract I was offered looked like clover.'

It has to be said that Granada have never paid super star fees to even the highest of the Street's earners. The programme would never have survived its first thirteen weeks if they had. But the £40 minimum fee they were giving to the main contract players in 1960 was generous and, more important, guaranteed regularly. In a precarious profession, no right-thinking unknown Equity member would have turned it down.

Anyway, Violet Carson by no means unknown, was only going to play hookey for five weeks – just to let the BBC know how well the

Violet Carson.

It took Count Basie's band in the next studio to do it, mind you. The silence that always preceded a 'take' was blasted by their music. The recording continued, with everyone hoping against hope that if the noise were heard on the tapes, viewers might mistake it for the Salvation Army passing by outside.

But it was too much for Miss Carson. The words dried on her lips, she raised her eyes in the general direction of heaven and informed the deity and anyone else who might be listening: 'I can't take any more!' No one had dared to throw such a spanner into the works since the Street first began. 'Stop tape,' called the director Howard Barker using those dreaded words for the first time in that studio.

Her attitude to noisy interferences had not changed since the day she had threatened to smack Tony Warren's bottom if he didn't keep quiet. Only this time it was Count Basie and his entire orchestra she was taking on.

Violet Carson died at the end of December 1983, aged eighty-five; Coronation Street, Blackpool and the nation mourned her.

Violet Carson as Ena Sharples with great grandson Jason, Sep. 1972.

'GRANADA were not mean with their offer'

opposition treated her. But they continued to treat her well for as long as she cared to stay. And she stayed to become one of the Street's abiding pillars. Her impact far outstripped her appearances, for she was by no means young and age, ill-health, plus the financial security of a lifetime's regular employment, had given her a crusty independence when she chose to show it. Yet she was fiercely proud of her place in the Street and the slightest hint that her protracted absence from the studio might give the impression she no longer wished to be part of it brought her magisterial presence into view at a trice, health permitting.

Her delivery of lines was the fastest in the business and the scriptwriters fell over themselves to make her volleys worth firing. She never failed them.

Well, hardly ever. There was one memorable moment during those early days of unbroken recordings from the beginning to end, when the word-gun backfired.

THE PRODUCERS

From the outset Coronation Street has been blessed with a succession of producers who have cared passionately about its contents and its quality. Men who have immersed themselves in the minutiae for its construction and its development, who have believed in its sense of reality.

Without these men whose talent is to know how the Street should feel from the inside, yet have the perception to stand back and judge it from the outside, Coronation Street would almost certainly not be still with us twenty-five years on.

It is the product of many different hands, many different minds and many different skills. But the producer is the keeper of its collective consciousness. Without his guiding hand the show is rudderless.

Two of the most constant forces with their hands on the tiller over the years have been Harry (H.V.) Kershaw and Bill Podmore. Harry Kershaw was in there right at the start as a writer when the Harries Elton and Latham were in overall charge.

Elton was a company executive so it was, in fact, Harry (Stuart) Latham who dealt with the day to day running of those first episodes.

But Harry Kershaw had no doubts that it was, in reality, the general spirit abroad within Granada itself which enabled those men to bring Tony Warren's brainchild to the screen as it was originally conceived.

'Granada was ruled by creative men to whom contracts and money were sordid companions in adventure,' he has said. 'I suggest that if Tony Warren had submitted Coronation Street to the ITV of the 80s, the programme would never have been made.'

Kershaw is a man who still has ideals when it comes to writing. He began his career in television after throwing up a safe, dull job in insurance, encouraged by Harry Elton's belief in his ability.

He worked alongside Tony Warren on those first batches of scripts, creating the run which followed on from Warren's original batch of twelve.

There is hardly a part of its creative process in which he has not in some way shared over the past quarter of a century.

'I count my blessings,' he once wrote, 'I have mixed writing and producing for Coronation Street for its first ten years. Since then I have been a regular contributor of scripts. It has given me a good living, an entrée into what is still an exciting world, an opportunity to place my work before Britain's largest audience and a chance to work as part of what I consider to be the best team in television. I hope they'll have me as long as I can hit a typewriter key.'

These days Harry Kershaw is more than content to hit his typewriter keys and leave the computer calculations of budgeting, balancing material resources with artistic needs, finding the talent and then affording to keep it, to others.

Those problems he is happy to leave to the programme's most enduring Executive Producer Bill Podmore and the man who has recently taken over the day to day production details, John Temple.

Podmore, as we know, is as Streetwise as it is possible to be in terms of this particular Street. He has been the producer and now Executive Producer of the series since 1976, coming in at a time when ratings were beginning to sag ominously; for the first time in its life it had failed to make the Top Twenty one week. His success can be judged from the fact that last Christmas both episodes of Coronation Street were in the top rated programmes in that most competitive of entertainment schedules, more than holding its own against the Queen's speech and the orgy of spectaculars and blockbuster movies which are pitched in to grab the captive audiences at home by the fire.

His approach is tough enough to earn him the nickname *The Godfather* of Coronation Street. If he feels the ends are justified, he allows no sentiment to stand in the way when it comes to protecting the ultimate wellbeing of the Street.

Yet sentiment plays an enormous part in his approach to his work.

Harry Kershaw – the first scriptwriter, later producer and contract writer.

John G. Temple – Producer 1985.

Like Harry Kershaw, he cares deeply about the end product, about the sound, the look and the feel of each episode. Like Kershaw, too, he has a nostalgia for its past. But it is a healthy, vigorous nostalgia that he uses as a guideline towards its future.

'I always said that the day we lost Ena Sharples was the beginning of the end for Coronation Street,' he told me. 'And yet now look. We've lost so many and yet, to me, I think the programme is still as potent as ever.'

Unlike Harry Kershaw, whose creative roots sprang from a love of drama and dialogue, Bill Podmore's training after leaving the RAF came first visually as a cameraman, then working his way through the labyrinth of television light entertainment. He adores the comic side of Street life.

This instinct he shares with the programme's latest producer John Temple who first graduated from Scottish light entertainment to Granada long enough ago to take over Tony Warren's desk in the promotions department in 1960. And as Warren had inherited the desk from Jack Rosenthal, one of the Street's most gifted early writers, Temple feels that there is something slightly pre-destined about his present post. He went on to become one of the programme's storyline writers before returning to Scotland as a producer.

Now he is back in what he regards as his second home, his plan for the future is to steady the ship after the buffeting winds of change it has just survived. 'I want to consolidate the characters we have. There are some very good new people we have to absorb. We can do that only so long as we remember that a great deal of the Street's appeal is its sense of family past. I'd like to hear the older generation sharing their reminiscences with the newcomers in the way Ena and Albert used to in the old days.'

Which of course means that Eric Rosser, the Street's official historian, will be once more working his way through his incredible filing system. Eric's involvement with the Street began when he had a long and painful stay in hospital after two fearfully crippling accidents. On a specially constructed TV set, originally used by Manchester United's star goalkeeper Bert Trautman after he had broken his neck, he'd watched the very first episode. And, with the compensation money he received, threw up his job in the tax office, bought a typewriter and started sending in script ideas. Purely as a hobby he also started to keep the files of data on each character. These are now the basis of his extraordinary system. There is not an incident, a date, a character nor an actor he cannot refer to. When the script insisted that Ken Barlow's son Peter was to enroll as a boy cadet, it was Eric who pointed out that the lad was underage ('But they insisted on writing the episode so I had to jiggle his birth date about a bit'). When George Waring was booked to play the role of Emily's bigamous husband, only Eric Rosser could instantly name the four other minor roles he'd already played in the Street.

'I have dossiers on everyone,' he says proudly. Like the rest, the Street is his job and his hobby and his life.

Bill Podmore – Executive Producer with Eric Rosser – Street historian.

*"If I had to choose between trophies
and a large, loyal audience,
I would always plump for the latter"*
— H. V. KERSHAW

INDEX

Page numbers in italics refer to illustrations.

ACKNOWLEDGEMENTS

The author would like to thank:
Eric Rosser
Leita Donn
Joan Riley
and all the Coronation Street production team at Granada for their whole-hearted cooperatio

The publishers wish to thank the following for their kind permission to reproduce the photographs in this book:
Express Newspapers Ltd 69 above; Mirror Group Newspapers 68 below; TV Times 16 above and below; Whitbread and Co plc.
All other material by kind permission of Granada Television.